PHILADELPHIA QUAKERS

A Brief History

William C. Kashatus

For Lauren Frances Baumann

Front cover image: "Sunday Morning in front of the Arch Street Meeting House, Philadelphia." Attributed to John Lewis Krimmel American (1786–1821), *c.* 1813. The Metropolitan Museum of Art, New York City. (*Public Domain*)

Back cover image: Colorized photo of Philadelphia Quakers, gathering at Arch Street Meeting House, *c.* 1891. (*Arch Street Meeting House, Philadelphia, PA*)

Fonthill Media Inc.
www.fonthillmedia.com
office@fonthillmedia.com

First published 2023

Copyright © William C. Kashatus 2023

ISBN 978-1-63499-498-9

Typeset in 10.5pt on 13pt Sabon
Printed and bound in England

Acknowledgments

I was introduced to Philadelphia Quakers in 1964 when I began my formal education at Frankford Friends School. There I met some of the most remarkable teachers who not only exemplified the integrity for which Quakers have been long known, but who cultivated my interest in Philadelphia's rich history and made a meaningful difference in my young life. It was the beginning of a sixty-year relationship with the Religious Society of Friends and one that continues today. For that, I am deeply grateful.

This book is dedicated to Lauren Frances Baumann, my niece and a fellow Earlhamite. She captured my heart as a little girl, restored my faith in Philadelphia Quakerism as a young adult, and, along with her husband, Doug, has provided our extended family with two beautiful children. Special thanks to the following individuals who reviewed earlier drafts of the manuscript: J. William Frost, emeritus professor of history and former director of Friends Historical Library, Swarthmore College; Randall Miller, emeritus professor of history, St. Joseph's University; Jean R. Soderlund, emerita professor of history, Lehigh University; and Michael Zuckerman, emeritus professor of history, University of Pennsylvania.

I also wish to thank the following individuals who granted the right to reproduce photographs: Sean Connolly, Historic Arch Street Meeting House; Ellen Endslow and Judy Ng, Chester County History Center; John Burkhart and Mike Petiti, William Penn Charter School; Mary Crauderueff, Quaker Collection, Haverford College; Jordan Landes, Friends Historical Library, Swarthmore College; Emily Smith, The Library Company of Philadelphia; Andrew Williams, Historical Society of Pennsylvania; Hoang Tran, Pennsylvania Academy of Fine Arts; Anne Burns, Westtown School; Kate Jiggins and Erin Betley, Lower Merion Historical Society; and Signe Wilkinson, *The Philadelphia Daily News.*

Finally, I am grateful to my parents, Balbina and William, for giving me the gift of a Quaker education, and to my wife, Jackie, and our three sons, Timothy, Peter, and Ben, who have brought tremendous joy to my life. My love for them is eternal.

Contents

Introduction

William Penn's statue stands atop Philadelphia's City Hall surveying a "Holy Experiment" fashioned from the principles of his Quaker faith. Clasping the royal charter to his colony in one hand, the English proprietor extends a blessing over his beloved city with the other. In a seventeenth-century world conditioned by violence, religious persecution, and arbitrary authority, Penn established a New World province dedicated to pacifism, religious liberty, and participatory government. No other society in western civilization came as close to realizing such utopian ideals as did Pennsylvania, with Philadelphia serving as its finest example. Even the name, the Greek derivation for "City of Brotherly Love," bore witness to Penn's sweeping vision of "what love can do if people united to achieve God's will on earth."

Unfortunately, few contemporary Philadelphians, and fewer visitors, know anything of William Penn or the Quaker religion that inspired the founding of his capital city. In fact, when asked whose statue adorns the French Baroque tower of City Hall, many residents mistake the figure as Benjamin Franklin, an eighteenth-century transplant from Boston who is Philadelphia's most recognizable personality due to his scientific genius, cunning statesmanship, and unparalleled talent for self-promotion.

Nor do contemporary Philadelphians know much about the many significant contributions the Religious Society of Friends made to the city's political, economic, and social culture. One of the reasons for this lack of knowledge is because Quakers found themselves in the minority of the population beginning in the early eighteenth century, and they continue to be among the smallest of the religious denominations in the Philadelphia area, which today encompasses the suburban counties of Bucks, Chester, Delaware, and Montgomery as well as the State of Delaware and southern New Jersey. Thus, when I reference "Philadelphia Quakers" in this book, I am also referring to these other regions.

Philadelphia Quakers have always exercised a disproportionate influence on local, state, and national affairs. They have been pioneers in social change, weaving the principles of religious liberty, racial and gender equality, conscientious objection, and civil disobedience into the legal and cultural fabric of the country. Friends established local institutions that made significant contributions to the fields of health care (Friends Hospital), business (Strawbridge and Clothier), industry (Lukens Steel), botany (Longwood Gardens), and especially education with three Quaker-founded colleges (Bryn Mawr, Haverford, and Swarthmore) and more than three dozen schools. Philadelphia is also the international headquarters of the American Friends Service Committee (AFSC), which was organized during World War I to staff battlefield ambulance units, rebuild war-ravaged villages in France, and feed impoverished German children after the conflict ended. Today, the AFSC continues to improve the living conditions for the needy and destitute at home and abroad by providing food, clothing, and shelter as well as medical care and working for peace among nations. The strength of Quaker leadership is that it arises from a genuine spirit of service to others and represents an earnest attempt to reach consensus among a group of people. This is the kind of moral leadership much sought after in our contemporary society.

Philadelphia Quakers: A Brief History was written by a Philadelphia Quaker for other Friends, residents of, and visitors to the City of Brotherly Love. As a product of the city's Friends schools, I became fascinated with Quaker history at an early age. That early fascination blossomed at Earlham College where my interest was nurtured by my professors. When I returned to Friends education as a religion and history teacher in the 1980s, I began researching, writing, and publishing essays on colonial Philadelphia. Later, as a graduate student at the University of Pennsylvania, I wrote my doctoral dissertation on William Penn's educational philosophy and the implementation of that philosophy in Philadelphia's Quaker and early public schools. Since then, I have written and published scholarly books on Friends' involvements in abolitionism, education, humanitarianism, and the peace movement.

Philadelphia Quakers provides readers with a narrative of the history of the city's Friends, beginning with the origins of Quakerism, a historically Christian sect, in seventeenth-century England and their relocation to the New World where they created a utopian colony under the leadership of William Penn in the 1680s. Organizing themselves into Philadelphia Yearly Meeting (PYM), the governing religious body of Quakers in southeastern Pennsylvania, southern New Jersey, and Delaware, Friends attempted to navigate the burning political and social issues they confronted during the next three centuries. In the process, Philadelphia Quakers struggled to remain true to their fundamental belief of an indwelling presence of God in all people and the related social testimonies of peace, community, equality, and simplicity.

In the eighteenth century, Friends struggled to defend their historic peace testimony while their non-Quaker neighbors went to war, most significantly against the French in 1756, and later against Great Britain in the War for American Independence between 1775 and 1783. Accused of cowardice or loyalty to the crown, Philadelphia Quakers, unable to reconcile their pacifist convictions with their duties to the public in wartime, withdrew from government *en masse* and suffered widespread persecution at the hands of the Continental Army and the Second Continental Congress, including the loss of property and even banishment.

After the American Revolution, Philadelphia Quakers, hoping to contribute to the welfare of the fledgling nation, became active in several humanitarian reforms. Friends became pioneers in abolitionism, women's rights, education, healthcare, and prison reform, and they continued their benevolent activities throughout the nineteenth century and well into the twentieth. At the same time, the city's Quakers experienced a painful religious schism.

The Great Separation of 1820s was caused by social, theological, and generational differences among Quakers and resulted in the division of PYM into Hicksite and Orthodox factions for more than a century. Property once held jointly was divided between the two branches, including meetinghouses and schools. While Friends continued their humanitarian activities, they tended to do so through separate organizations with the Orthodox joining non-Quaker reformers and the Hicksites self-segregating within their own branch. Friends of both branches also continued to advocate for peace and social justice during the Civil War.

The Industrial Revolution brought new challenges. While Friends criticized the excesses of capitalism and the social vanities that accompanied it, many of them rose to prominence in business. Quaker benevolence reflected the same paradox during this time. Friends were generous with their time and money towards black freedmen and Native Americans but were ambivalent towards the suffering of the immigrant masses in their own city. Instead, those Friends who embraced the Social Gospel supported the temperance movement, civil service reform, and women's suffrage. They also founded the American Friends Service Committee (AFSC) during World War I and focused on the issues of conscientious objection, alternative service, and rebuilding war-torn Europe, efforts they continued during World War II. In 1955, the Hicksite and Orthodox factions resolved their differences and reunited in a single yearly meeting. During the next half century, Philadelphia Quakers provided a meaningful education to

Friends and even greater numbers of non-Friends through their schools and colleges. They continued to promote peace and participate in relief work abroad through AFSC. They also furthered the cause of social justice at home through the various committees of PYM, weekend work camps, and the Friends Council on National Legislation (FCNL).

Today, however, Philadelphia Yearly Meeting is confronted by declining membership and a significant loss of leadership in their constituent monthly meetings, outreach programs, schools, and colleges. Unless this trend is reversed, Friends will become irrelevant in a city that is plagued by poverty, gun violence, racial discrimination, and failing schools—a city that needs them more than ever before. Hopefully, this book will inspire the current generation of Philadelphia Quakers to reclaim the virtuous example of earlier Friends who shaped the history of our city, and spread their message of peace, religious freedom, and brotherly love around the world.

William C. Kashatus

1

Quaker Origins

Quakerism was born in the smoldering cauldron of religious and political turmoil that gripped mid-seventeenth-century England. In an age when there was no separation of church and state, the arbitrary authority of the monarch created bitter resentment within parliament and among the many non-conformist religious sects that existed. The hostility resulted in a decade-long military confrontation pitting the crown against the Commons.[1]

Between 1642 and 1651, a civil war was fought between the Anglican supporters of King Charles I and parliament's Puritan forces under the command of Oliver Cromwell. Although the Puritans sought to purify the Church of England by ridding it of Roman Catholic practices, the fundamental issue underlying the conflict was the future of England's government and the degree to which the monarchy and elected representatives would hold power. When the Royalist army was defeated in 1648, Charles I was charged with treason and beheaded a year later. The war ended in 1651 when Charles's son, Charles II, fled to France, temporarily ending the Stuart monarchy. England was declared a commonwealth under the rule of a Puritan-dominated parliament. But after Cromwell dissolved that body in 1653, he became lord protector of England, Scotland, and Ireland, acting simultaneously as head of state and head of government.[2]

Terrified by the Puritan doctrine of man's utter depravity and encouraged by Cromwell's policy of religious toleration, the common people increasingly turned to new religious sects. There were the Anabaptists, who rejected infant baptism, oathtaking, and the payment of church tithes. Another sect, the Seekers, emphasized personal spiritual inspiration over the authority of a formal clergy. Ranters shared these ideas, but also believed in the divinity of any strong emotion and that they were immune to sin. Other sects infused their religious beliefs with utopian ideas. The Levelers, for example, preached absolute social and political equality. The Diggers were more radical, hoping to establish a democratic government based on scripture. They also believed that the land should be free to all people and tried to launch their utopia by digging up common property and planting carrots. Even more fanatical were the Fifth Monarchists, who believed that the Kingdom of God was about to come and that they should hasten its arrival by overthrowing the British government.[3]

While none of these sects survived, they did introduce many of the ideas absorbed by the Quakers, who emerged from the same tumultuous climate. That Quakerism did survive is largely due to two exceptional individuals: George Fox, who founded the sect and held it together despite the widespread persecution suffered by hundreds of members; and William Penn, who rescued the non-conformist group from further persecution by establishing a New World colony with a very advanced form of government. Remarkably, both individuals were relatively young, being in their twenties and thirties, when they made their unique—and invaluable—contributions to the fledgling Quaker movement.

George Fox (1624–1691) was a religiously inspired tradesman from Northern England and the individual who founded the Religious Society of Friends. The son of a Leicestershire weaver, Fox had been unusually sensitive to God as a youngster. Initially, he turned to local ministers and relatives to fill his spiritual void. Unable to resolve the dilemma, Fox resorted to reading the Bible and prayer, often in solitude.[4] Occasionally, he received "openings," or insights he believed were inspired by God, such as "a university education is not needed to preach the Word of God," and that "the people are God's true church."[5]

Quaker founder George Fox (1624–1691). (*Library of Congress*)

Not until 1647—when Fox, at age twenty-three, began traveling the English countryside preaching and working as an itinerant shoemaker—did he resolve the spiritual turmoil that raged inside him. According to his *Journal*, the epiphany came in the form of a "small voice within," that said: "There is one, even Christ Jesus, that can speak to thy condition."[6] Fox's discovery of Christ as a present reality served as a powerful motivation to continue his itinerant ministry. Preaching in marketplaces, open fields, and even at churches at the close of the service, Fox exhorted seekers to "heed the voice of Christ within," a concept known as the "Inner Light."[7]

Rejecting the Puritan beliefs of original sin and eternal predestination, Fox claimed that the individual could achieve salvation on their own by turning inward for divine guidance, rather than relying in an outward intermediary such as a priest or minister. He preached that God endowed each person with a divine spark, or "Inner Light," that allowed them to communicate directly with the Lord. This Inner Light was not an intellectual or theological concept as much as it was a "living experience" within each person and one that compelled the individual to "do good."[8] As a result, Fox encouraged his followers to "wait in the Light for Wisdom," then to use that wisdom to lead a "Christ-like life" and to "walk cheerfully over the world answering that of God in others."[9] In other words, seekers, inspired by God's leading, would be honest in their business dealings, compassionate to the needy, and gentle, loving and peaceful to everyone. Quaker worship was also conditioned by these principles.

Early Quakers, like Puritans, regarded the Anglican Church as corrupt and renounced its formal services and rituals. To that end, they established a simple form of worship, meeting in fields and homes and later plain meetinghouses devoid of an altar, statues, or any other adornments. Worship was conducted in silent meditation in order to "wait upon the Lord" for divine inspiration. In the process, members of the gathering attempted to repress the natural self and enter a communion with God and with each other using the Inner Light as a vehicle. Once inspired, a member might stand and share a prayer. Others might quote a favorite Bible verse. Still others would deliver a spiritual message he or she received. Ideally, the same messages would reach members simultaneously. The "meeting for worship" ended with a simple handshake symbolizing the intention of each member to go out into the larger society and act on the Friends' unique beliefs.[10]

Historians identify 1652 as the beginning of the Quaker movement. During the spring of that year, Fox traveled to Westmoreland and Lancashire, in the North of England, which was home to a large group of spiritual Seekers, much like he had been. There, he climbed up a small, desolate mount called "Pendle Hill" and saw "a large people to be gathered."[11] These Seekers would become known as the "Children of the Light," or "Friends of the Truth," references to the Gospel of John 1:9, "the true light that lighteth every man that cometh into the world." Later, the name was simply shortened to "Friends."[12]

Fox's early converts were known as the "Valiant Sixty," though they numbered closer to seventy men and women. These were the first Quaker missionaries, itinerant preachers who spread the sect's beliefs across the British Isles during the second half of the seventeenth century. Many of the early Quakers were ordinary farmers and tradesmen. But the movement also attracted the wealthy and well-educated including Robert Barclay, a Scottish scholar who became the first Quaker theologian; William Penn, the Oxford-educated son of an admiral in the king's navy; and Margaret Fell, the wife of a prominent judge who allowed their home of Swarthmoor Hall in Ulverston to be used as the headquarters of the movement. In 1659, a decade after Judge Fell died, George Fox married Margaret, who played critical roles in financing the Quaker movement and interceding with legal authorities on behalf of those Friends who were imprisoned for their beliefs.[13]

Regardless of wealth, class, or education, the early Quakers embraced a unique set of social testimonies. For example, they refused to doff their hats to honor those in positions of authority because they believed that in God's eyes all people were of equal worth. Only in the presence of God, they believed, should a Quaker remove his hat. Similarly, Friends refused to swear oaths on a Bible in court because it suggested a double standard, one in their daily lives and the other when they were under oath. Quakers insisted on a single standard of behavior that was consistent with Christ's injunction, "Swear not at all … let your communication be yea, yea, or nay, nay." Friends also gave women a more equal status than anywhere in the English-speaking world, allowing them to be recorded ministers. They used the familiar "thee" and "thou" when speaking to others, instead of the deferential "you," and dressed in plain black, gray, and drab white clothing to demonstrate a life devoted to Christian simplicity.[14]

These peculiar testimonies and the Friends' utter devotion to them gave integrity to the Quaker faith, but also challenged the established Church of England and underscored the sect's conscious disregard for all expressions of social class distinction. Such disregard was dangerous in a seventeenth-century society that operated on rigid class differences. Although Fox had no desire to establish a religious sect—only to proclaim what he saw as the genuine principles of Christianity in their original simplicity—he did assume a leadership role. He was effective because of his dynamism and the intense personal experience he was able to project.

Once, during a court hearing at Derby in 1650, the judge, named Bennet, mocked Fox's exhortation to "tremble at the word of the Lord," calling him and his followers, "Quakers." It was an insulting label, suggesting that Fox and his adherents were unstable and intent on turning the world upside down. But the offensive moniker was later adopted as a pseudonym for the Society of Friends.[15] Judge Bennet sentenced Fox to six months in jail for "preaching his blasphemous beliefs." Offered release if he would accept a commission in Cromwell's army, Fox refused, saying that he "lived in the virtue of that life and power that takes away the occasion of all wars." For this he was jailed another six months.[16]

To be sure, not all early Friends were pacifists. Pacifism was initially a matter of individual conscience. Like the other social testimonies adopted by Quakers, the peace testimony evolved over time. Accordingly, many early Friends believed that the English Civil War was a manifestation of God's desire to purge evil within human hearts which removed the cause for warfare.[17] This so-called "Lamb's War" was a reference to Christ who is the Lamb in the Book of Revelation. Thus, some early Friends joined Cromwell's Army in order to affect the Kingdom of God on earth. Not until 1660 when the Stuart monarchy was restored did pacifism become a fundamental article of the Quaker faith. Suspected of being members of the Fifth Monarchists, a fanatic sect determined to overthrow the government, Fox and other early Friends presented *A Declaration from the Harmless & Innocent People of God Called Quakers* to Charles II:

[This assured him that the Quakers] utterly deny all outward wars, strife and fightings with outward weapons for any end or under any pretense whatsoever; this is our testimony to the whole world: The Spirit of Christ, by which we are guided, is not changeable, so as once to command us from a thing as evil, and again to move us unto it; and we certainly know, and testify to the world, that the Spirit of Christ, which leads us into all truth, will never move us to fight and war against any man with outward weapons, neither for the Kingdom of Christ nor for the Kingdoms of this world...[18]

At a time when political and religious conflicts were decided by warfare and common men were required to serve in the military, the peace testimony was tantamount to treason. Unwilling to compromise their religious beliefs and social testimonies, Friends were persecuted under the Quaker Act of 1662 and the Conventicle Act of 1664, which also targeted other non-conformist groups. Some historians estimate that as many as 15,000 of England's 60,000 Quakers had been imprisoned by 1689 when an Act of Toleration was finally passed by parliament. Of that number, more than 450 Friends died of torture, including public whippings, the pillory, branding, and imprisonment.[19] The cruelest case was that of

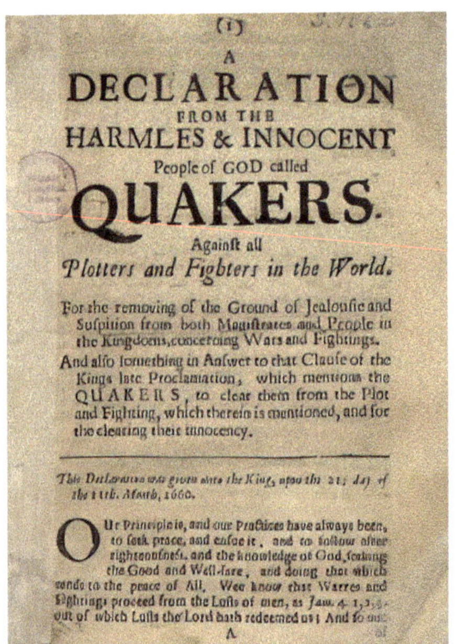

Declaration of Friends to King Charles II of England, 1660, commonly known as "the peace testimony." (*Library of Congress*)

James Nayler, a member of Fox's Valiant Sixty who was found guilty of blasphemy and imprisoned. Not only was Nayler pilloried, flogged, and branded on his forehead with the letter "B" for blasphemer, but his tongue was bored with a hot iron to prevent him from ever preaching again.[20]

Fox and his wife, Margaret Fell, repeatedly petitioned the king for the release of Friends who were imprisoned to spare them further torture. Fox himself suffered severe persecution being thrown down church steps, beaten with sticks, and imprisoned eight times during his life. Occasionally, the strain gave way to erratic behavior. Once, after a long imprisonment, Fox had a vision of blood flowing through the marketplace of Lichfield, a city neighboring his native village of Fenny Drayton. It was the dead of winter, and Fox felt compelled to walk in stockinged feet through the streets of the city crying, "Woe to the bloody city of Lichfield." Initially puzzled by the experience, he eventually deduced that the vision of blood related to the "thousand martyrs in Lichfield in the Emperor Diocletian's time." "I must go in my stockings through the channel of their blood in their marketplace," wrote Fox in his *Journal*. "So I might raise up the blood of those martyrs that had been shed more than a thousand years before."[21]

While George Fox founded Quakerism and provided the personal magnetism, moral courage, and raw energy to attract others to the new religion, William Penn saved the fledgling movement and gave it respectability. He did so by writing voluminously to defend Quaker beliefs and by using his legal understanding, personal finances, and connections

James Nayler (1618–1660) had the letter "B" for "blasphemer" branded on his forehead by English authorities for preaching his Quaker beliefs in violation of parliament's Conventicle Act. (*Public Domain*)

at the royal court to establish a North American colony as a sanctuary from the religious persecution Friends suffered in Europe.

William Penn (1644–1718) came from a world of privilege and great turmoil. Born on October 14, 1644, Penn was the eldest of three children of Margaret and Sir William Penn, a wealthy admiral in the Royal Navy. Like other members of the petty aristocracy, the admiral wanted his son to secure a position at the royal court. As a result, young William enjoyed the advantage of an exceptional education. At the elite Chigwell Grammar School, he was introduced to the classics and mastered both Latin and Greek. At age sixteen, Penn entered Christ Church College, Oxford University, as a gentleman-commoner. This status was reserved for those whose sole purpose was to gain the necessary connections to secure a position at the royal court, rather than scholarship, which was intended for those entering parliament or the clergy. But the young Penn gravitated to academia and began to question the ethics of his aristocratic upbringing as well as the teachings of his Anglican faith. During his third year at the university, Penn joined a group of other students who refused to attend mandatory chapel services and conducted prayer meetings of their own. The revolt resulted in the expulsion of the dissident group from Oxford.[22] When Penn returned home, his father "beat and whipped [him] and drove [him] from the house," according to the diarist Samuel Pepys, who was a neighbor. Only his mother's pleadings spared him from being disinherited.[23]

Disappointed in his son, Admiral Penn sent him off on a grand tour of the European continent, another prerequisite for the education of a young member of the petty aristocracy. Penn became proficient in French history and culture. His frequent contact with the court of Louis XIV introduced him to the upper echelons of royal society. While the elder Penn hoped that his son would conform to the expectations of his privileged background, young William found greater appeal in pursuing religious studies at the Huguenot Academy in Saumur, France. There he met and studied with Moise Amyraut, a prominent French theologian. Penn also witnessed the ability of the French Huguenots to practice their faith under the Edict of Nantes. The Huguenot experience of religious liberty was at the time rare in Europe, with the French monarchy tolerating the worship of any religious group contrary to the state-supported church.[24] This experience would later influence Penn's ideas in establishing a New World colony.

Meanwhile, the political climate in England had changed. By 1660, Cromwell's Puritanism had been rejected, and the Stuart monarchy was restored to the throne. Charles II, back from exile in France, turned his attention to the subjugation of the Catholics in Ireland and confiscating their lands when they refused to pay exorbitant rents. Penn's father, who was promoted to vice admiral under Cromwell, had been rewarded for his military success with a confiscated Irish estate near Cork called Macroom Castle. Shifting his political allegiance, the English naval commander now courted favor with Charles II and his brother, James, duke of York, a Catholic.[25] Despite the peaceful coexistence of Anglicanism and Catholicism at the royal court, parliament enacted a series of repressive religious measures known as the Clarendon Code. Not only did the new law elevate the Church of England to established church status, but also declared nonconformist religious observances to be illegal. Among the dissenting groups were the Quakers.

In 1664, Penn, age twenty, returned from France "a most modish person in dress and a gentleman," according to the diarist Samuel Pepys.[26] After a brief time at Lincoln's Inn in London where he studied law, Penn entered the military and was sent to Ireland to manage his father's estate and to settle a property dispute over some new lands Charles II had given his father. At the time, the British government was establishing a uniformly Protestant empire in Ireland. English landlords were driving Irish Catholics from their native soil while parliament made it illegal for them to practice their faith. In the midst of all the turmoil, Penn put down an insurrection of troublesome soldiers at Carrickfergus. He even sat for a portrait in a suit of armor, one of just two known likeness of Penn that still exist.[27]

It appeared as if the Admiral's hopes for his son were coming to fruition. But England's unjust treatment of the Irish had a profound effect on Penn,

King Charles II reigned over England from 1660 to 1685. Engraving by William Holl, *c.* 1830. (*Public Domain*)

William Penn (1644–1718) had planned to become a courtier as a young man and dressed the part by donning a suit of armor. Engraving by Jean-Baptiste Adolphe Goupil, Paris, *c.* 1897. (*Library of Congress*)

who began to waver in his loyalty to the Stuart monarchy and the Church of England. Although he was offered the captainship of his own regiment, Penn declined the post choosing instead to manage his father's Macroom Castle estate.[28] The turning point in Penn's life came two years later, in *c.* 1666–67, when he heard the preaching of Thomas Loe.

Loe was an itinerant Quaker minister who often preached at the marketplace in Cork. Attending a meeting of Irish Quakers one day, Penn was deeply moved by Loe's message that "there is a faith that overcomes the world and works by love, not by violence; a faith in which zeal and charity are companions." "This Quaker bid me ... to not to satisfy [myself] with outward things [like] a position or a title, but with an inward faith," wrote Penn in an account of his convincement a decade later. "His words spoke to my condition and ... with a great opening of joy, I became a Quaker."[29]

During the next year, Penn sought out Quaker meetings, absorbed himself in the literature written by Friends, and gained a strong understanding of the Quakers and their religious convictions. He also experienced the same persecution they endured for their refusal to obey parliamentary measures that outlawed nonconformist groups and the teachings of the Anglican Church. When he learned of his son's conversion to the despised religious sect, the admiral ordered him home immediately and begged him to reconsider fearing it would bring dishonor to the family as well as ruin his son's chances to secure a position at the royal court. Penn struggled with the decision, not wanting to disappoint his father while also being drawn to this new religion.[30] Unable to make a complete break with his past, the aspiring courtier asked George Fox how long he should continue to wear his sword. "Wear it as long as thou canst," replied the Quaker founder, leaving the decision to Penn's own conscience.[31] Ultimately, William told his father that he could not abandon his commitment to the Society of Friends. Saddened and angered by the decision, the admiral disinherited his son. Although Penn had distanced himself from his father, he also remained a product of his upbringing, enjoying the privileges of wealth, education, and a high social status.[32] Those advantages would eventually bring respectability to the despised religious sect.

Between 1667 and 1680, William Penn was a fierce defender of the Quaker faith. He wrote several treatises defending his new religion, including the *Sandy Foundation Shaken*, which denied the doctrine of the Trinity. The pamphlet earned him the wrath of the bishop of London, who charged him with blasphemy and jailed him in the Tower of London for nine months.[33] In another tract, *No Cross, No Crown*, Penn advocated the "elimination of pomp and ceremony" in religious rituals in favor of "genuine faith and virtuous simplicity."[34] Jailed in Newgate prison in 1670 for violating a law

Sir William Penn (1621–1670) was a British admiral and father of William Penn. Engraving by Samuel Woodburn, London, 1841. (*Public Domain*)

that prohibited Quaker worship, Penn wrote *The Great Case of Liberty of Conscience*, which argued that "liberty of conscience" is not "a mere liberty of mind" but the freedom to "exercise" religion. Penn insisted that civil restraint and religious persecution carry an "evident claim of [civil] infallibility" and "enthrones man as king of conscience."[35] He also persuaded a jury to acquit him of any wrongdoing. Angered by their decision, the judge imprisoned the jurors for two months. Refusing to be intimidated, the jurors, after their fines were paid, regained their freedom. In the process, they won for all English juries the right to make decisions without fear of reprisals and Penn gained the stature of a "martyr" among Friends.[36]

During this time, Penn also married Gulielma Springett, the stepdaughter of another influential Quaker. Settling outside of London, the couple began a family that eventually grew to three children: William, Jr., Springett, and Letitia. Penn also continued to write voluminously and travel throughout the British Isles and the European continent spreading his fervent Quaker beliefs.[37] Just as important, Penn, in 1670, reconciled with his father who was on his deathbed.[38] The reconciliation was vital to the survival of Quakerism, more than Penn realized at the time.

Because of their distinctive religious practices and their rejection of the established Anglican Church, British Friends continued to suffer widespread persecution. Thousands were forced to pay fines or arrested and imprisoned. Forced to sleep on cold floors in dimly lit, poorly ventilated prisons for months on end, Quakers were often abused by overzealous guards or fellow inmates. Local meetings were organized to record the sufferings of Friends, to raise money for their legal defense and for the needs of itinerant ministers. These gatherings evolved into monthly meetings for business while local meetings for worship met on a weekly basis.[39] Realizing that the very survival of their movement was at stake, Friends began to consider the possibility of immigrating to North America to escape the religious persecution.

Quakers had journeyed to the New World as early as 1656 when Ann Austin and Mary Fisher arrived in Boston, Massachusetts. Banished by Puritan authorities who feared that they would persuade their congregants to desert the established church, Austin and Fisher relocated to the Quaker colony in Barbados. One year later, Robert Fowler, a Quaker convert from Bridlington, England, and eleven other Friends sailed on the ship *Woodhouse* and settled in Rhode Island. From this base, Friends like Mary Clark, John Copeland, Mary Dyer, Christopher Holder, and Humphrey Norton embarked on missionary trips to the Massachusetts Bay colony to make other Quaker converts.

Despite repeated fines, whippings, imprisonment, and the October 27, 1659 hanging of Mary Dyer on Boston Common, Puritan authorities were unable to prevent the increasing numbers of Friends from entering New England. Instead, Quakerism spread from Massachusetts into Maine, New Hampshire, and Connecticut. Several Quaker communities sprang up in New York at Mamaronek, Westchester, Purchase, New Milford, and Nine Partners and then spread along the southern seaboard into New Jersey.

Even Quaker founder George Fox himself visited the American colonies in 1672–73, attending meetings in Maryland, New York, Rhode Island, and New Jersey. Months later, when Fox returned to England, he met with William Penn to tell him about the vast unsettled territory in the mid-Atlantic region. Accordingly, Penn's initial involvement in the New World came in 1674 when he was asked to arbitrate a land dispute between John Fenwick and Edward Byllinge, the two Quakers who established the West Jersey colony.[40] When the legal struggle resulted in the bankruptcy of both Friends, Penn, as a creditor, became one of many Quaker proprietors of the colony. *The Concessions and Agreements of 1677*, signed by Penn and 150 others, mostly Quakers, established representative government in West Jersey as well as the civil liberties of the settlers, and provided a model for Penn's later Frame of Government. By 1682, 1,760 Quakers settled in West Jersey.[41] Penn, impressed by the rapid growth, began to consider the possibility of his own Quaker colony.

In 1680, Penn petitioned Charles II for a New World colony as payment for the 16,000-pound debt the crown owed his late father for military service against the Dutch. For Charles, it was a wonderful deal. Not only would he be paying off a long-standing debt, but he would also rid England of the troublesome Quakers and the other non-conformist groups to which Penn opened his colony. After a year's negotiation, the king, on March 4, 1681, made Penn the proprietor of a New World colony granting him a charter for 45,000 square miles of land in North America, a parcel that was almost as large as England itself.[42] As proprietor, Penn enjoyed full governing rights over the colony. He controlled how land was gained and dispersed, how the cities and towns were to be plotted and populated, and how the government, its laws, and public institutions were to be organized. Charles insisted that the colony be named in honor of the admiral and Penn complied naming it "Pennsylvania" or "Penn's Woods."[43] The new proprietor spent the next year promoting his colony in Great Britain and Europe and making plans to insure its economic and political stability.

Penn appealed to the king's brother, James, duke of York, to grant his colony access to the sea in order to establish a vital trade network with England. James complied by deeding him the additional three "Lower Counties," which now comprise the state of Delaware.

Penn also sent his cousin, William Markham, to Pennsylvania to take possession of the land and to serve as a liaison with the scattered English, Dutch, and Swedish groups who had already settled there. Penn promised these settlers that he would "not usurp the right of anyone" and

James, duke of York (1633–1701). Engraving by Nicolas Bocquet from Horace Walpole, *A Catalogue of the Royal and Noble Authors* (4 vols., 1806), Volume I, p. 158. (*Public Domain*)

that they would be "governed by laws of your own making."[44] To fulfill his promise, the new proprietor drafted a First Frame of Government that guaranteed the right of all settlers to worship as they pleased and established a government in which all freemen (i.e., white, Protestant male landholders over the age of twenty-one) participated. Although he targeted the Quakers as his primary group of settlers, Penn opened his colony to all non-Quakers as a haven from the religious and political persecution they had experienced in Europe. To this end, he launched a vigorous recruitment campaign across the British Isles and on the European continent. He genuinely desired that Pennsylvania operate on the most virtuous principles of toleration, justice, and brotherly love and that God had inspired his mission.[45]

"For my country, I eyed the Lord in obtaining it, and … owe it to His hand and power, than in any other way," Penn wrote to James Harrison, a prospective settler on August 25, 1681. "I have so obtained it, and desire that I may not be unworthy of His love, but do that which may answer His kind Providence, and serve His Truth and people; that an example may be set up to the nations … for such a holy experiment."[46]

For more than two decades, William Penn had dedicated his life to the principles of religious freedom and the liberty of conscience. At age thirty-eight, Penn was now ready to transform those principles into a "holy experiment" in his New World colony of Pennsylvania.

2

William Penn's Holy Experiment

On August 30, 1682, William Penn set sail for the New World. Departing from Deal, England, Penn sailed on the ship *Welcome* captained by Robert Greenaway, a London Quaker.[1] On board were about 100 men, women, and children. Most were members of the Religious Society of Friends who had been persecuted for their nonconformist beliefs, either in England or Ireland. Other passengers were Baptists, Presbyterians, and at least two members of the Church of England. Among the prospective colonists were merchants, farmers, white indentured servants, and a variety of tradesmen, including tanners, brewers, weavers, and carpenters.[2]

The three-month voyage was miserable. The 300-ton vessel had an overall length of 108 feet, a keel of 76 feet in length, a breadth of 27½ feet, a depth of 17 feet, and a draught of 10½ feet, making living conditions crowded and noisy.[3] Each passenger brought his own food to be prepared and cooked as best he could. But the crew's diet was limited largely to brined beef, dirty water, and cracker-like biscuits. The sharply salted food and meat and foul water resulted in dysentery, constipation, scurvy, and mouth rot in addition to other physical maladies. An epidemic of smallpox killed as many as thirty-one passengers. Penn, who was immune because he suffered the illness as a child, nursed the sick. Nor did the unpredictable weather help matters. For two or three nights, the ship fought gale-force winds and piercing rains. Many feared for their lives as the ship was rocked by the storms and damaged by crushing waves.[4] Somehow the *Welcome* survived the treacherous voyage, becoming the first of a fleet of ninety-one ships that carried an estimated 7,200 immigrants to Pennsylvania within the next three years.[5]

In late October, Penn saw his New World colony for the first time. He could not help but be impressed with its rich forests of oak, beech, maple, pine, and tulip poplar. Smaller trees, bushes, and shrubs covered

The ship *Welcome* carried William Penn and about 100 passengers across the Atlantic to Pennsylvania between August 31 and October 27, 1682, completing the Atlantic crossing in fifty-seven days, which was slow by seventeenth-century standards. Sketch by unknown artist, 1912. (*Public Domain*)

the ground, along with many species of wildflowers. The forests were abundant with wildlife, including white-tailed deer, pheasants, foxes, rabbits, and squirrels. "The air is sweet and clear," Penn later wrote in promotional descriptions of his colony, "the heavens serene, like the South part of France."[6]

Nor was Penn the first to arrive in the colony. Many native tribes had preceded him, including the Erie, Honniasont, Huron, Iroquois, Leni Lenape, Munsee, Shawnee, and Susquehannock, among others. The Dutch were the first Europeans to lay claim to the land in 1609 when explorer Henry Hudson sailed into the Delaware Bay. Ten years later, Dutch trading posts were established in the region. In 1638, the New Sweden Company established the colony of New Sweden at Fort Christina in present-day Wilmington, Delaware. When Governor Johan Prinz arrived in 1643, he built two forts at Tinicum Island in present-day South Philadelphia, thereby establishing the first permanent European settlement in the region. Angered by the Swedes' claim, Dutch troops under the command of Governor Peter Stuyvesant of New Amsterdam (New York) seized control of the Swedish colony in 1655 and held it until 1664 when the British duke of York claimed the land. When Penn was granted his charter in 1681, he was not fully aware of the cultural conflict in his colony, but he believed that whatever tensions existed needed to be resolved in a peaceable manner. To that end, Penn sent his cousin, William Markham, ahead of him to present his deed of ownership as well as a proclamation instructing the Dutch and whatever Swedes remained to transfer their allegiance from the duke of York to him.[7]

Landing at New Castle (present-day Delaware) on October 28, Penn met with the Dutch and Swedish inhabitants. To his relief, both groups gladly acknowledged him as their new proprietor and promised their allegiance. The next day, Penn sailed up the Delaware River to the Swedish village of Upland (present-day Chester), where he hoped to establish his capital. But after meeting with William Markham, his cousin and deputy governor, he learned that all of the habitable waterfront was occupied by the Dutch, Swedes, or English and that they were demanding high prices for their real estate.[8] As a result, Penn looked for another location, eventually deciding on a sparsely settled peninsula at the confluence of the Schuylkill and Delaware rivers.

Penn had already named his capital, "Philadelphia," the Greek derivation for "City of Brotherly Love," and designated it as one of Pennsylvania's original three counties, along with Bucks and Chester. Philadelphia would become the cornerstone of a utopian colony based on the Quaker ideals of religious toleration, participatory government, and pacifism.[9] At a time when European society was characterized by religious intolerance, the arbitrary authority of monarchs, and seemingly endless warfare, Penn's vision of a colony where settlers could worship as they pleased, participate in government

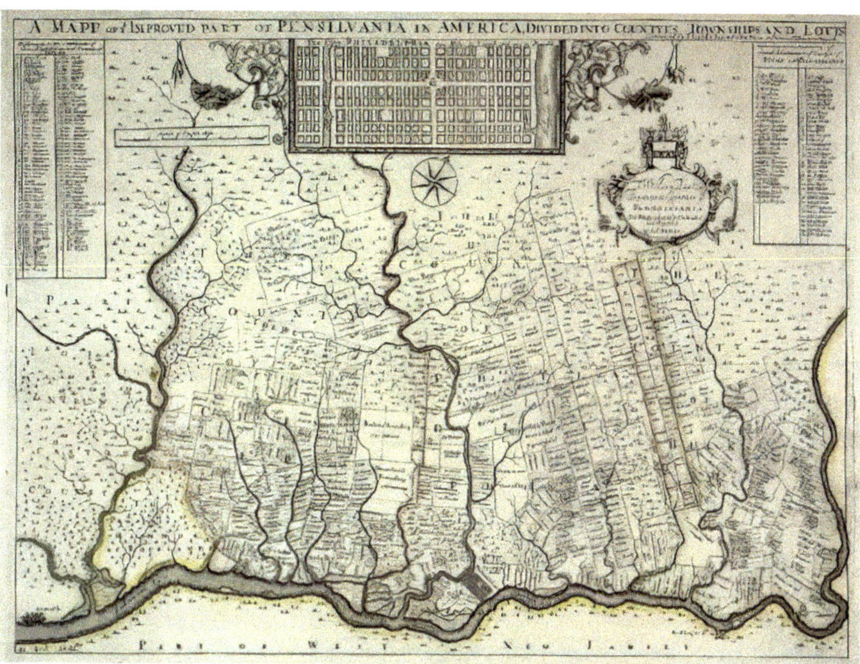

Thomas Holme's 1681 Map of Pennsylvania showing rural landholders' names and lots located in the Philadelphia area. The City of Philadelphia with its checkerboard layout can be seen at the bottom center near the confluence of the Schuylkill and Delaware rivers. (*Library Company of Philadelphia*)

affairs, and live in peace and harmony with each other was truly unique. So unique that Penn referred to his province as a "Holy Experiment."[10]

The term "holy" indicated Penn's firm belief that God had given him the colony to create a haven for religiously persecuted peoples, and that the success of the enterprise would glorify the Lord. But Penn's reference to "experiment" had a dual meaning, both in the seventeenth-century Quaker interpretation of a "religious experience" as well as in the modern sense of a "trial." Penn viewed the granting of his colony as a providential gift from God and as a sign of the approaching millennium. Since the land came from God, Penn believed that he had an obligation to "serve His truth and people so that an example may be set up to the nations."[11] Thus, the Quaker proprietor, in a religious sense, hoped that his colony would be a life-changing experience for those who settled there. In a political sense, however, Penn also considered his colony a place where he would experiment with religious toleration, self-government, pacifism, city planning, and universal education.[12]

First and foremost, Pennsylvania would be an experiment in religious toleration. Penn guaranteed settlers the freedom to worship and he believed that this experiment would succeed because of his great faith in human nature. For Penn, human nature was improvable, but only if the individual accepted the direction of the inner light. At the same time, he was confident that humans would be responsive to the indwelling presence of God because he viewed them as rational creatures whose ability to reason would bring them closer to God.[13] "Reason, like the sun, is common to all and brings all men to the same light, whether they be Christian or non-Christian," he wrote in *Sandy Foundations Shaken* (1668).[14] Such a positive view of human nature, based on both Quaker and Enlightenment principles, informed Penn's belief that all people could become virtuous members of society if liberty of conscience was protected by government. Liberty of conscience was sacred to him. To persecute any individual because of his religious beliefs not only threatened the liberty of all people but was also an offense against human nature because it contradicted the reason and inner light with which God endowed every person.[15] Having suffered persecution himself, Penn was determined to guarantee the liberty of conscience in his province in his Frame of Government (1682).

Predictably, Pennsylvania attracted hundreds of religiously persecuted peoples from across Europe, including Quakers from the British Isles; French Huguenots; Irish Catholics; Lutherans from Catholic German states; Swiss, Amish, and German Mennonites; as well as members of other religious sects.[16] Such inclusivity was unique among North American colonies. The Puritans, who established New England a half-century earlier, stressed social homogeneity and religious uniformity, excluding those not of the same mind.[17] Their emphasis on exclusivity was grounded in a view of human nature as tainted by utter depravity. Only a minority of the elect were predestined for salvation, and they comprised the leadership of colonial New England.[18] Roman Catholics tried to create religious toleration in Maryland under the leadership of Lord Cecil Calvert in 1654, but they were overthrown in 1689 when the Glorious Revolution of William and Mary prevailed in England. Three years later, in 1692, the Maryland Assembly established the Church of England as the official religion of the colony and Maryland's experiment with religious toleration ended.[19] Entrepreneurs seeking to enrich themselves by exploiting the natural resources of the land settled in the southern colonies of Virginia and the Carolinas. Although they came from a variety of faiths, religion was a secondary concern.[20]

But Penn's understanding of religious freedom must not be confused with the modern definition of the term, which insures civil liberties to all, regardless of faith. His Frame of Government restricted the right to vote and to hold political office to those who believed in God and Christ. He denied those rights to Jews and Muslims, who did not believe in Jesus Christ as savior. For these groups, like other non-Protestants in the colony, "religious toleration" meant that they were only free to worship and practice their faith.[21] Nor did Penn's plans for a religiously and socially diverse society preclude his desire to create a prosperous economy or his personal financial concerns.

To recoup the considerable expense that he had invested and to realize a profit, Penn encouraged "three sorts of people" to settle in his colony. The first group was composed of 600 purchasers of 5,000 acres or more. These "First Purchasers" provided the seed money to establish the colony. In return, Penn promised to reserve 10 acres of land in Philadelphia for each 500 acres purchased. But he stipulated that purchasers seeking 1,000 acres or more would have to settle a family on each 1,000-acre lot within three years. He also encouraged the purchasers to bring servants by offering a bonus of 50 acres, with an annual quitrent due to Penn of 4 shillings for each servant settled in the colony. The second group was comprised of some 4,000 yeoman and farmers who would join Penn in establishing the province between 1682 and 1684. These emigrants belonged to religiously and politically persecuted groups, including the English, Dutch, Scotch-Irish, German, and Welsh, both Quaker and non-Quaker. Although these groups possessed little capital to invest, they would be an important source of revenue for Penn who would charge them quitrents for the land. He would also rely on this group to transform the wilderness into a prosperous economy. Indentured servants made up the third and final group. They agreed to work for a period of years in exchange for their passage to Pennsylvania. At the end of their service, each one would receive 50 acres of land. During the interim, however, indentured servants would be the backbone of labor in the colony.[22]

Second, Pennsylvania was an experiment in a more democratic form of government than existed in Europe. Blending religious principle with contemporary political theory, Penn's Frame of Government promised the settlers "a voice in government, the right of trial by jury, and the liberty of conscience," though the right to hold office was limited to freemen (i.e., white, male landowners over the age of twenty-one who were also Protestant). Participatory government, like religious toleration, was also based on the Quaker proprietor's positive view of human nature.[23] "Government, like clocks, go from the motion men give them," he wrote in the preface to his 1682 constitution. "And as government are made and moved by men, so by them they are ruined, too. Let men be good and the government cannot be bad. If government becomes ill, good men will cure it."[24] To ensure that "men were good," and prevent corruption, Penn organized his government into three parts: a governor, initially himself, who supervised the distribution of land, negotiated with the Lenape Indians, and initiated legislation; a provincial council of seventy-two members, mostly Quakers, which proposed legislation; and a bicameral legislature of up to 500 members, evenly divided between Quakers and non-Quakers and elected by the people, which voted to approve or reject legislation. The constitution gave tremendous independence to the provincial council and established the governor as a powerful executive. At the same time, Penn's Frame of Government was also the first constitution to provide for peaceful change through amendments. A proposed amendment required the consent of the governor and 85 percent of the elected representatives.[25]

Benevolent though Penn was, the freemen became disgruntled over his executive power as governor and proprietor and constantly pressured him for greater political authority. Penn reluctantly granted a Second Frame of Government in 1683 which gave the freemen the authority to propose legislation.[26] Nevertheless, the dominant role Friends played in the colony was reinforced by the fact that many prominent Quaker merchants held leadership positions in the assembly as well as in Philadelphia Yearly Meeting (PYM), the main governing body of Friends in Pennsylvania, New Jersey, and Delaware. Though technically separate from the civil government, PYM exercised considerable influence in these geographical areas, which were organized into several quarterly meetings, which in turn were composed of multiple monthly meetings (similar to congregations).[27] Nevertheless, Pennsylvania's experiment in government not only set a precedent for religious freedom, but also furthered the principles of popular sovereignty and the separation of powers. These innovations were adopted by the Framers of the U.S. Constitution a century later.[28]

Third, Pennsylvania was an experiment in brotherly love. Penn broke with the earlier English precedent of volatile relations with Native Americans by extending his friendship to the Delaware tribes in his colony and purchasing their land instead of seizing it by warfare. Unlike the Iroquois who inhabited the lands to the north, the Lenni Lenape, the tribe who lived in scattered villages along the Delaware river, were a peaceful people who hunted, fished, and farmed the land they inhabited. They preserved their political sovereignty by negotiating peace with the Dutch and Swedes, avoiding extended war through diplomacy and trade.[29] Penn speculated that Lenape were "of the Jewish race," or "of the stock of the Ten Tribes" of Israel and as such were children of God and entitled to love and respect.[30] As a result, Penn, in a letter to the Lenape prior to his arrival, expressed his intention to "enjoy the land with your love and consent so that we may always live together as neighbors and friends."[31] While Penn recognized the Native Americans' right as legal owners of the land granted to him by King Charles II, he did insist that they give their consent to his occupation of it. He also made an official policy of his government to purchase the land from the Indians, thereby extinguishing native title before any land was patented to white settlers.[32]

William Penn making a peace treaty in 1683 with Tamanend, a chief of the Lenape ("Delaware") Indians, under the shade of an elm tree near the village of Shackamaxon (now Kensington) in Philadelphia. Engraving by John Hall, London, 1775, after the original painting by Benjamin West, 1772. (*Public Domain*)

According to legend, Penn, in 1683, met with Lenape chiefs to express his intentions. Realizing that the tribe preferred to meet outdoors so that the heavens could witness their interactions, he agreed to gather under a large elm tree at Shackamaxon, about a mile north of Philadelphia. Here, the proprietor promised his new Indian neighbors fair treatment, an opportunity for a redress of their grievances, and, above all, peaceful relations. The Lenape chiefs made a similar pledge. There were no signatures, no oaths, or formal documents of the agreement, just a heartfelt promise that the French philosopher Voltaire would call the "only treaty between the Indian nations and the Christians that was not ratified by oath, and was never broken"—at least in Penn's lifetime.[33]

To ensure his treaty with the Lenape, Penn established a list of conditions for both the colonists and the Quaker officials for their conduct in dealing with the Indians. Among these concessions were sharing the land, trading goods of the same quality sold in the marketplace, and trial by jury. Although the latter provision was not practical because the Indians did not understand it, or necessarily agree to submit to colonial authority in settling disputes, the concept did indicate Penn's sincerity in dealing with them.[34] Penn's idealism had its limits, though.

While he believed that Native Americans were the spiritual equals of white men, Penn did not consider them of the same intellect. "These poor people are under a dark night in things relating to religion," he wrote in a 1683 *Account of the Lenape*. He was especially put off by their worship, which consisted of animal sacrifice and dancing around a fire while singing and shouting: customs he considered "savage."[35] Predictably, Penn refused to grant the Lenapes the right to vote or to hold political office in his colony. Like Jews and Catholics, Native Americans did not enjoy religious freedom in the modern sense of the term.

Nor did Penn extend the protections of his charter to enslaved Africans and African Americans either. Indeed, the proprietor kept at least three slaves at Pennsbury, his country estate in Bucks County, north of Philadelphia. He considered these slaves his property, part of his personal estate—not human beings. He also knew that his colony's prosperity depended on slavery.[36] Thus, Penn, if he had any reservations about human bondage, kept them to himself when, in 1688, Francis Daniel Pastorius (a young German attorney) and three other Quakers belonging to Germantown Meeting outside of Philadelphia drafted a petition to abolish slavery in the colony. "Is there any man who would [want] to be sold or made a slave for all of his life?" began the anti-slavery petition:

There is a saying that we shall do to all men like as we will be done ourselves; making no difference of what generation, descent or color they are.... Here is liberty of conscience which is right and reasonable; here ought to be liberty of the body.... But to bring men hither, or to rob and sell them against their will, we stand against....

If we shall do to all men like as we will be done ourselves, what worse thing can be done towards us, than if men rob or steal us away, and sell us for slaves to strange countries; separating husbands from their wives and children? We who profess that it is not lawful to steal, must, likewise, avoid purchasing such things as are stolen, but rather stop this robbing and stealing.[37]

After Pastorius presented the anti-slavery petition at the local monthly meeting at Abington on April 18, 1688, it was sent on to Philadelphia Quarterly Meeting, where it was again considered before being sent on to Philadelphia Yearly Meeting. It appears that none of the meetings wanted to pass judgement on such a "weighty matter," realizing that it would have a far-reaching effect on Pennsylvania's economic future. Instead, the Yearly Meeting minutes noted that the petition would be sent to the London Yearly Meeting for further consideration, though no direct evidence exists that they did. Nevertheless, the *Germantown Petition* was the first of its kind in North America and laid the groundwork for a slow but growing abolitionist movement among Philadelphia Quakers.[38] Thus, William Penn, for all his idealism, was a product of his time, conditioned by the political and social conventions of the seventeenth century.

Fourth, Philadelphia was an experiment in city planning. Having lived through the devastating Great Fire of London in 1666, Penn took great care in planning the design of his capital city.[39] Avoiding the narrow streets and densely packed houses that had fueled London's catastrophic fire, the Quaker proprietor directed his surveyor-general, Thomas Holme, to create an urban center that reflected the principles of order and symmetry.[40] Holme divided the 2.3-square-mile city into four quadrants. Two main thoroughfares, Broad and High (later Market) Streets, intersected at a 10-acre "Centre Square" that was reserved for a "House for Public Affairs," or city hall. Additional squares were set aside in each quadrant for public recreation. Streets that ran north to south were numbered and those that ran east to west were named after local trees, such as Mulbery, Chestnut, Walnut, Spruce, and Pine. Each house was situated in the center of an assigned lot, "so there may be ground on each side for gardens, or orchards, or fields."[41] This orderly pattern established a precedent in city planning and ensured the "greene country towne" Penn had intended.

Finally, Philadelphia became the laboratory for an experiment in education challenging the seventeenth-century notion that schooling was the responsibility of the family, church, and local community. At the time,

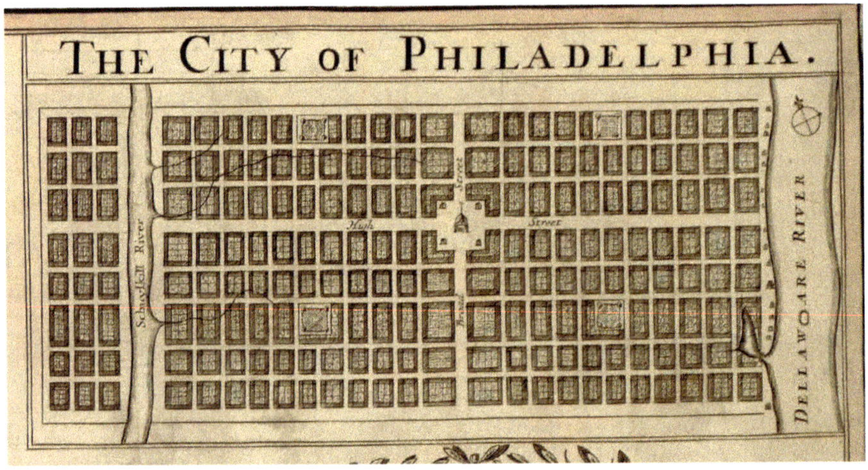

In 1682, Thomas Holme, surveyor-general of Pennsylvania, laid out Philadelphia as the "greene country towne" that Penn envisioned. The original city stretched two miles east to west across a tract of land situated between the Delaware and Schuylkill Rivers. Holme designed an orderly grid plan with streets organized around a large square in the center of the town and four smaller squares, one in each quadrant. The grid also included two main streets, Broad and High (present-day Market), which were kept wide in hopes of preventing the kind of fire that destroyed London in 1666. Facsimile taken from Thomas Holme, *A Portraiture of the City of Philadelphia, 1683. (Public Domain)*

children learned informally through observation and discipline in the home, attendance at church, and apprenticeship in a trade.[42] While New England Puritans established a Latin school in Boston, Massachusetts, to prepare children for a higher education which would train them for the ministry, Penn, arguably the most enlightened educational theorist of his time, saw the need for a practical and moral education. He urged that learning be "liberal" but consist of "useful knowledge, such as is consistent with Truth and Godliness."[43]

Penn directed his provincial council to join with Philadelphia Monthly Meeting and establish a separate educational institution to educate all the children in his colony "to the age of twelve," regardless of religion, wealth, or gender.[44] Founded in 1689 and incorporated in 1698, the "Friends Public School" taught children the "rudiments of literacy" and apprenticed them to a trade at age thirteen. Penn hoped that such "a virtuous education of youth" would cultivate the principles of religious toleration, participatory government, and brotherly love.[45] In so doing, the school would provide his colony with honorable leadership and constructive citizens committed to his utopian vision.

In later years, Penn revised the school's 1698 charter to meet the changing demographics of the colony. In 1701, for example, government

Founded in 1689 and called the "Friends Public School," Friends Academy moved to the east side of Fourth Street, just south of Chestnut Street in Philadelphia in 1744. Situated next to the Fourth Street Meeting House, the school remained at this site for nearly a century, until 1841. Engraving by William L. Breton, 1829. (*William Penn Charter School, Philadelphia, PA*)

sponsorship of the school was abandoned due to concerns about the union of church and state. Similarly, in 1708, Penn eliminated Philadelphia Monthly Meeting's governance, placing the school under the care of a board of overseers. He removed the requirement that all overseers be Friends in 1711. While the majority of overseers continued to be Quaker, not all the teachers belonged to the Society of Friends.[46] In these ways, the Friends Public School met the needs of a growing—and diverse—population.

By the beginning of the eighteenth century, Philadelphia was a growing city of 2,200 residents. A town hall, courthouse, and a marketplace, as well as a Quaker Meeting House, dominated the urban landscape. In addition, some 400 red-brick houses were clustered on the eastern side, although 1,200 acres separated the Delaware and Schuylkill rivers marking the eastern and western boundaries of the city. Many of the urban dwellers were English Quaker merchants and artisans, who controlled Philadelphia's economic and political culture. While Welsh Baptists, German Lutherans, and Scots-Irish Presbyterians also inhabited the city, they, along with pietist groups like the Amish and Mennonites, tended to settle outside the urban limits. Most of these non-Quaker groups were farmers who established the villages of Bustleton, Byberry, and Oxford to the northeast, and Haverford, Merion, and Radnor to the west.[47] Regardless of their residency, all of the groups benefitted from Quaker business connections in England and the West Indies.

Philadelphia quickly became the cornerstone of the mercantilist trade that defined the economic relationship between Britain and her North American colonies. The surplus wheat, flour, and grains harvested on the fertile farmlands surrounding the city were brought to port where they were shipped to the West Indies for sugar and molasses. The profits from those commodities were used to purchase manufactured goods in England and imported back to Philadelphia. As the mid-Atlantic trade grew, there was a greater demand for artisans, including the shoemakers, tailors, and weavers.[48] Together with the colonial merchants and mechanics, Philadelphia's artisans formed an industrious middle class that initiated the city's economic expansion as the eighteenth century unfolded.

If William Penn had had his way, he would have remained in his New World colony to supervise the government and mediate any disputes that arose between the various peoples who settled there. But after his initial visit in 1682–84, he became an absentee landlord who governed through several lieutenants. Forced to return to England in 1684 to resolve a boundary dispute with Maryland, Penn expected to return to his province within a year's time. Instead, his absence stretched over a fifteen-year span during which he suffered both personal and professional tragedies. His beloved wife, Guli, died in 1694, leaving him the widowed father of their three surviving children, William Jr. and Letitia. Although he remarried and his new wife, Hannah Callowhill, the daughter of a wealthy Quaker merchant, provided him with three more children, Penn never fully recovered from the death of his first love. His financial affairs were also in disarray due to the delinquency of many settlers who refused to pay the quitrents they owed him. Penn's own excessive spending and mismanagement of his properties added to his financial woes.[49] There were other problems, too.

During Penn's extended absence, Philadelphia Yearly Meeting (PYM), the governing body of Friends in the colony, witnessed a schism. The disagreement was initially about the relationship between the historic or human and divine Jesus and the emphasis Friends placed on the Inner Light—the belief that everyone was given Inner Light by God—as opposed to formal traditional faith in Jesus Christ. The conflict began when George Keith, a Scottish Quaker and the headmaster of the Friends Public School, challenged the authority, discipline, and organization of PYM. Keith proposed a reorganization of the Yearly Meeting's discipline, including compulsory doctrinal tests about belief in Christ for Quaker membership, the removal of automatic birthright membership, and a new system of elders. His proposals ignored the existing hierarchy of Quaker ministers and monthly, quarterly, and annual meetings, which were generally dominated by wealthy Quaker merchants who often held dual roles as church leaders and civil magistrates—another point of contention for Keith who believed that no Quaker minister had a right to sit as a civil magistrate. When separate Keithian Meetings, called "Christian Quakers," were established, PYM disowned those Friends who joined them.

Keith never attracted more than a small minority of Friends. His movement dwindled until the 1720s when some of his followers sought to rejoin PYM, and formally acknowledged they had been at fault for going "into separation." Others migrated to other denominations, mainly the Anglicans and the Baptists. Keith himself eventually left Quakerism and joined the Church of England. However, the issues he raised have reappeared in every major Quaker schism since the seventeenth century.[50]

Problems also arose between the Quakers, who administered the government, and the non-Quaker settlers. There were heated disagreements over land distribution and rental fees, political patronage, the Quaker monopoly of commerce, and Penn's inability to govern effectively because of his absence from the colony. When he finally returned in 1699, he was besieged by demands to revise the constitution. Seeking refuge at Pennsbury Manor, an 8,400-acre country estate he had built 26 miles north of Philadelphia on the Delaware River, Penn met with members of the legislature at his courtly Georgian-style manor house, trying to arrive at a solution that would satisfy the non-Quakers settlers. He concluded that he had no other choice but to give more political power to the inhabitants of his colony.[51]

On October 28, 1701, Penn issued a new constitution, called the Charter of Privileges, to salvage his Holy Experiment. He appeased the assembly and the quarrelsome settlers by creating a unicameral legislature with powers unknown elsewhere in the colonies. The Charter reaffirmed the assembly's right to draft legislation, choose its speaker and other officers, and "exercise all other powers and privileges of an assembly according to the freeborn subjects of England." It also limited the role of the provincial council to an advisory capacity and eliminated the governor's power to suspend or dissolve the assembly, though Penn could continue to veto legislation. No other colonial assembly enjoyed so much power. No other governor was so clearly pitted against a legislative body. It was the exact opposite of what Penn had wanted when he established Pennsylvania two decades earlier. At the same time, the Charter of Privileges enhanced the principle of self-government, and preserved Penn's steadfast commitment to religious toleration.[52] Fifty years later, in 1751, the Pennsylvanian Assembly had a bell cast to commemorate the Charter of Privileges.

Around the crown was inscribed the biblical phrase, "Proclaim Liberty thro' all Land to all the Inhabitants Thereof—Levit. XXV 10." The 2,080-pound bell was raised in the State House steeple and became known to history as the "Liberty Bell."[53]

Penn spent the remaining two decades of his life in England defending his proprietorship against parliamentary threats to take control over Pennsylvania and make it a royal colony. Deeply in debt due to failed investments, a high standard of living, and financial mismanagement, Penn had mortgaged the colony to an unscrupulous business manager, Philip Ford, who tricked him into signing over many of his proprietary holdings. After Ford's death in 1702, his heirs attempted to collect the huge debt owed to his estate.[54] Penn offered to sell his colony to the crown to settle the dispute and negotiations continued until June 1712 when he received an initial payment of £1,000 from the British government. But the transfer of the colony to the crown was never completed.[55]

On October 4, 1712, Penn suffered a debilitating stroke. His wife assumed responsibility as acting proprietor and head of government, becoming in practice though not in law the first female governor of Pennsylvania. Working with a series of deputy governors, Hannah Penn

The Liberty Bell was commissioned by Speaker Isaac Norris of the Pennsylvania Assembly in 1751 from the Whitechapel Foundry in London. The bell was hung in the tower of the Pennsylvania State House and commemorated the fiftieth anniversary of William Penn's 1701 Charter of Privileges which granted religious liberties and political self-government to the people of Pennsylvania. Engraving appeared on cover of *Graham's Magazine*, June 1854. (*Public Domain*)

managed all of the province's official business and bailed her husband out of personal financial debt. Her accomplishments were considerable. Not only did Hannah maintain peaceable relations with the Lenape, Conestoga, and Iroquois Indian tribes, she also prevented the outbreak of civil war between Pennsylvania and Maryland over an on-going boundary dispute and lessened the political dissension that existed in Pennsylvania's assembly.[56]

After Penn's death on July 30, 1718, Hannah thwarted attempts by her irresponsible stepson, William, Jr., to contest his father's will and lay claim to the province as head of the family. Although William, Jr. died before the case was settled, his son, Springett, tried to have the court declare the will invalid, asserting that his grandfather was mentally incompetent when he wrote it. But Hannah prevailed, ensuring that her children received the estate. When she died on December 20, 1726, the proprietorship of Pennsylvania passed to her three sons: John (1700–1746), Thomas (1702–75), and Richard (1707–71).[57]

William Penn's success in establishing a society based on the principles of religious toleration, participatory government, and brotherly love was exceptional for a man of his wealth and aristocratic background. His progressive vision enabled him to anticipate many of the defining aspects of a free society, including religious liberty, popular sovereignty, and cultural diversity. In so doing, Penn provided a blueprint for the Framers of the U.S. Constitution. But he was not a man without shortcomings.

Like many idealists, Penn was more of a visionary than an administrator. If he had paid closer attention to his financial affairs, he would not have accumulated the considerable debt that nearly cost him his proprietorship.[58] If he had taken a more active role in the government of his colony, he may have avoided the political squabbles between the Quaker-dominated assembly and the non-Quaker settlers, which resulted in a new constitution that diminished his authority as governor. Perhaps most tragic was the fact that Penn paid considerably more attention to public affairs than personal ones. If Penn had spent more time nurturing his sons, inculcating the same Quaker principles he valued, and preparing them to become responsible leaders of the government, he might have insured the success of his colony for future generations.[59]

Sadly, Penn's heirs were irresponsible proprietors whose insatiable desire for financial gain led to the decline and fall of their father's beloved Holy Experiment.

3

A Peaceable People

Philadelphia's steady economic growth during the first half of the eighteenth century led to the rise of a Quaker merchant aristocracy who were well-fixed financially and socially. The acquisition of great wealth was based, in part, on involvement in a lucrative transatlantic slave trade and a provisioning trade with slaveholding plantation colonies in the Caribbean. These enterprises resulted in a laxity of religious discipline and a temptation to indulge in luxury and ostentatious living.[1] Even the education offered by the Friends Public School had become elite, catering to the children of wealthy Friends and emphasizing a classical curriculum, rather than the practical course of fundamental literacy and moral instruction upon which the school was established.[2]

Quaker involvement in Pennsylvania government was also coming into conflict with the Society of Friends' peace testimony, as non-Quaker settlers increasingly lobbied the assembly for a militia. By 1756, with the outbreak of the French and Indian War, financial prosperity and political expedience had compromised the fundamental integrity of Quaker faith and practice. The disturbing trend aroused a new generation of Friends to champion a spiritual reformation based on a return to the early Quaker testimonies on pacifism, simplicity, and equality.[3]

Having secured the leadership of Philadelphia Yearly meeting, the reformers believed that Quakerism had not yet become a firm tradition to be preserved and defended. It was still evolving. As problems arose, rules of discipline as reflected in written advice needed to be modified to meet those problems. This was especially true in the 1750s after PYM initiated reform among its members.[4]

The origins of the spiritual reformation can be traced to the irresponsible governance of William Penn's own sons, who became absentee proprietors of Pennsylvania after his death in 1718. Choosing to live in England,

Thomas, Richard, and John Penn governed the colony through lieutenants and milked the province for their personal financial gain. Having renounced their Quaker birthright to join the more fashionable Church of England, the Penn brothers did not share their father's commitment to peaceful relations with the Delaware Indians. They expropriated native lands in order to accommodate the westward migration of English, German, and Scots-Irish colonists. To this end, they enlisted the support of James Logan, a member of the provincial council and William Penn's secretary who had been entrusted by Penn to deal fairly with the Indians.[5] In 1737, Logan conspired with Thomas Penn, then governor, to cheat the Indians out of their tribal lands in an infamous event that is known to history as the "Walking Purchase."

Thomas claimed to possess a 1686 deed from the Lenape chief Mechkilikishi granting his father all the Indian lands that "a man could walk in a day and a half" from Wrightstown in Bucks County. Although William Penn and Mechkilikish understood the distance to be about 30 miles, Thomas, desiring land above the 30-mile limit, hired two runners to make the "walk" in record time. As a result, the "Walking Purchase," which took place in September, covered more than 60 miles. With Thomas Penn's permission, Logan used the same ploy to seize more than 1,000 square miles of Indian territory, forcing the Delaware to relocate to the Wyoming Valley near present-day Wilkes-Barre.[6]

Again, in 1754, the Penn family collaborated with the powerful Iroquois by "purchasing" the remaining Delaware tribal land in western Pennsylvania. But this time the Delaware would not go quietly. The French, at war against England, seized the opportunity to take control of North America and its lucrative fur trade by playing upon Indian grievances against the proprietors. After the defeat of British redcoats at Fort Duquesne, the defrauded Indians, at the urging of their French allies, attacked several white settlements in order to reclaim their lands. The Delaware killed and scalped dozens of men and forced their captured wives and children into slavery. White settlers sought revenge launching their own attacks and committing similar crimes. The bloody atrocities marked the end of the Quaker peace policy.[7]

When appeals for military assistance by the Scots-Irish settlers were ignored by the Quaker-dominated legislature, the aggrieved frontiersmen condemned the body as "cowardly sons of bitches." Then they loaded their dead onto carts, drove them to Philadelphia, and left them in front of the State House doors. Later, Scots-Irish settlers to the west, known as the Paxton Boys, took up arms against the natives. They killed members of the peaceable Conestoga tribe and sent others fleeing to Philadelphia for protection, only to march on the city and threaten the government.

Left: James Logan (1674–1751) served as governor of Pennsylvania in the 1730s and broke with William Penn's policy of friendly relations with the Lenape Indians by forcing them to vacate their lands in the Upper Delaware and Lehigh valleys. Engraving by unknown artist, *c.* 1740. (*Public Domain*)

Below: Map of Walking Purchase, 1737. Initiated by William Penn's sons, the Walking Purchase swindled the Lenape Indians out of 1,200 acres of their tribal land along the northern reaches of the Delaware River. (*Author*)

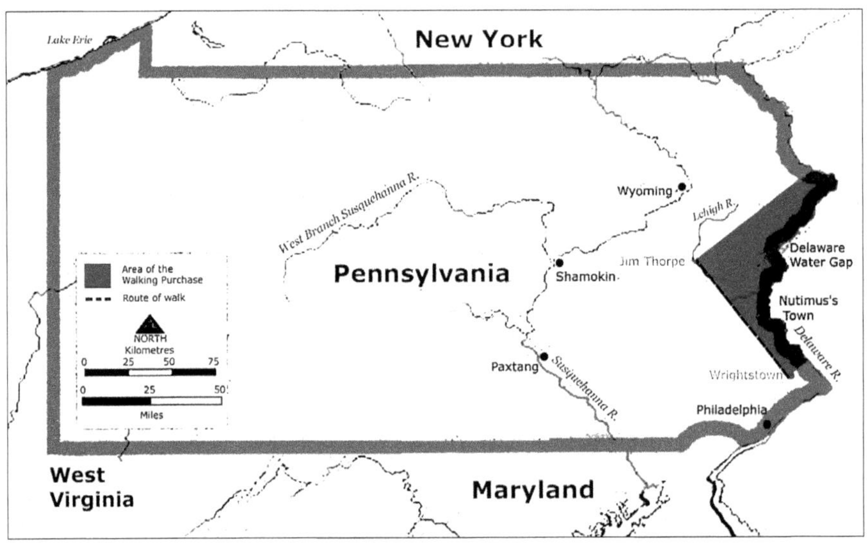

Yielding to public pressure, Pennsylvania Governor Robert Morris, in April 1756, declared war on the "Indian rebels and traitors," placing the Quaker-dominated assembly in an impossible position.[8]

Israel Pemberton, Jr. (1715–1779), known as "King of the Quakers" due to his leadership in the legislature as well as in Philadelphia Yearly Meeting, opposed the declaration of war and refused to appropriate funds for the defense of the frontier.[9] Pemberton and the other Quaker pacifists in the assembly were accused of sacrificing the lives of their non-Quaker neighbors to the west. Other Quaker politiques like Isaac Norris, II (1701–1766), the speaker of the assembly, attempted to blend their religious convictions with the practical ways of the world by supporting defensive warfare. But the majority of Quaker assemblymen resigned their seats unable to reconcile their responsibilities as public officials and their pacifist beliefs.[10] Many of these Quakers later organized the "Friendly Association for Regaining and Preserving Peace with the Indians."[11] Thus, control of the legislature passed into the hands of an Anglican-Presbyterian coalition which raised a militia and waged war against the French and their Indian allies.

The division between Philadelphia's Quakers and non-Quakers was a manifestation of a much larger problem—the political instability of the colony itself. Since 1726 when William Penn's sons assumed control of the province, they antagonized a more liberal anti-proprietary faction in the assembly. Initially, their differences centered on paying quitrents and a balance of power in the legislature. By the 1760s, however, both groups struggled openly for control of the government. Matters came to a head in the spring of 1764 when the assembly adopted a petition to King George III to assume control of the colony. The petition was a shrewd political coup by the anti-proprietary "Quaker Party," a coalition of Quakers and Moravians led by Benjamin Franklin. Franklin, an independently wealthy inventor, newspaper editor, and legislator, was a shameless opportunist who hoped to enhance his own fame, fortune, and political power by unseating the Anglican and Presbyterian assemblymen who controlled the proprietary interest.[12] In the process, Franklin seized power from Speaker Isaac Norris, head of the Quaker Party, who resigned from the assembly. Despite Franklin's machinations, the Proprietary Party, led by John Dickinson, won a sweeping victory in the fall election, and retained control of the government.[13] It was a temporary victory, though.

Increased British taxation with the passage of the Stamp Act in 1765 mobilized Philadelphia's Quaker merchants, who opposed the act by signing a non-importation agreement.[14] Parliament repealed the Stamp Act to end the violent protests led by non-Quaker colonists. But even this relative peace disappeared in 1767 with the passage of the Townshend Acts on British tea, paper, glass, lead, and china. While the few Quaker officials who remained in

Satirical cartoon depicting Benjamin Franklin mocking Quakers for their hypocrisy. At left, Abel James, a prominent Quaker merchant, hands out tomahawks to Native Americans from a barrel. At right, Israel Pemberton, clerk of Philadelphia Yearly Meeting and a Quaker legislator, embraces a bare-chested Native American woman, who steals his pocket watch. At center are a group of four pacifist Quakers with sad faces, holding beer mugs and pipes, sit around a tavern table discussing the growth of "the Paxton spirit" in the frontier and the political influence of the Presbyterians. Unknown artist, 1764. (*Library of Congress*)

the Pennsylvania Assembly tried to curtail public opposition to the acts, they were unable to contain the radical factions who encouraged violent opposition to British taxation. With the outbreak of war in 1775 and the subsequent publication of the Declaration of Independence a year later, Philadelphia Quakers realized that the situation could not be resolved without physical violence. That same month, Franklin and the so-called "Quaker Party" overthrew the conservative Penn proprietorship and instituted a radical new constitution driving out the few Quakers who remained in the assembly.[15]

Philadelphia Yearly Meeting not only condemned the War for American Independence, but it discouraged members from joining the Continental Army and from paying "any fine, penalty, or tax, in lieu of their personal services for carrying on war or supported a militia" in violation of the peace testimony.[16] The decision phlaced Philadelphia Quakers in an impossible position. On one hand, PYM received nearly unconditional support from London Yearly Meeting in negotiating with the British government for exempting its members from serving in a militia. On the other, the refusal to support the war effort resulted in persistent accusations that Quakers were loyal to the British crown.[17] In fact, the response of individual Friends to the American Revolution varied widely.

Some Quakers remained staunchly loyal to the British government. Others supported the patriot cause. Young Friends were swept into the war viewing it as a struggle for freedom and volunteered to fight for the Continental Army. Older Friends sympathetic to the patriot cause supplied the army with food, clothing, or military intelligence, paid war taxes, or participated in relief efforts by tending to the wounded after battles or comforting American prisoners of war.[18] Their efforts often resulted in disownment from PYM.

Between 1775 and 1781, 948 members were disowned from Philadelphia Yearly Meeting, 515 for miliary deviations, 165 for paying fines and taxes, 144 for taking loyalty oaths to the new government, thirty-two for assisting the war effort, and twenty-two for various deviations such as watching military training exercises and celebrating American independence.[19] The numbers of disowned included the Free Quakers who elevated the liberty of conscience above the peace testimony and genuinely believed that the revolution would usher in a freer society and one blessed by God.[20] The Free Quakers, who established their own meeting after the war, included some of the most prominent names in Philadelphia Quakerdom: Elizabeth Claypoole Ross (1752–1836), later known as "Betsy Ross," the seamstress who allegedly made the first American flag; Timothy Matlack (1730–1829), who, as clerk of the Second Continental Congress, inscribed the original Declaration of Independence on vellum; Lydia Darrah (1729–1789), a spy for General George Washington; and Owen Biddle (1737–1799), a prominent merchant who fought for the Continental Army. Like many of those Friends who supported the patriot cause in non-combatant ways, these "Fighting Quakers" were disowned by Philadelphia Yearly Meeting for violating the peace testimony.[21]

However, the majority of Friends remained neutral in the conflict and often suffered for their pacifist beliefs at the hands of loyalists and patriots alike. Some were arrested by the state's revolutionary government for refusing to pay taxes or follow conscription requirements. The most extreme case occurred on September 4, 1777, when Pennsylvania's Executive Council ordered the arrest of nineteen Quakers, many of them leaders of PYM, who were considered a "security threat" for collaborating with the British. Rejecting writs of *habeas corpus* to produce evidence of the charges against them, the patriot government exiled the group to Winchester, Virginia, without a trial. Many became seriously ill and two died during the hard winter months.

Several Philadelphia newspapers sprang to the defense of the Quaker exiles, but the Executive Council silenced the criticism. Not until April 1778, when Elizabeth Drinker (1735–1807) and several other wives of the exiled Friends confronted George Washington, commander of the Continental Army, was something done to alleviate their suffering. Initially, Washington stated that he could do nothing for them, refusing to interfere with the proceedings of a state government, but he eventually conceded granting the exiles special permission to pass through enemy lines and return home to Philadelphia.[22]

Substantially more Quakers experienced economic hardship due to the seizure of their property by the British, who occupied Philadelphia from September 26, 1777, to June 18, 1778. "How insensible these soldiers appear taking blankets, horses and food, while our land is so greatly desolated, and death and sore destruction has overtaken and impends over so many," wrote Elizabeth Drinker in her wartime journal.[23]

When the Americans returned, the situation did not improve. Now it was the Continental Army that plundered the homes of the pacifist Friends. Worse, a special court established by the Executive Council of Pennsylvania found two Quakers—Abraham Carlisle and John Roberts—guilty of treason for "knowingly and willfully aiding the enemy" and hanged on November 7, 1778.[24] PYM's Meeting for Sufferings cared for Friends who suffered from persecution by both governments. But even the Meeting for Sufferings could do little to protect Friends from the anti-Quaker vitriol of angry mobs who damaged and looted their homes when American troops regained Philadelphia after the British occupation of the city.[25]

Between 1756 and 1781, the gradual abandonment of Quakers from Pennsylvania government and the persecution of Friends by non-Quakers for their refusal to support that government in wartime resulted in a spiritual reformation within Philadelphia Yearly Meeting. Friends increasingly distanced themselves from the larger non-Quaker society and became a "peculiar people" dedicated to the unique social testimonies of their faith: simplicity, equality, community, and pacifism. Accordingly, PYM required all members to return to a primitive simplicity in behavior and lifestyle. Friends were strenuously urged to rid themselves of "vain customs of the world" such as wearing ostentatious clothing and participating in music, theater, and art. Marriage outside the Society of Friends was also discouraged and often resulted in disownment. Parents insisted that their children not associate with non-Quakers fearing that they might be "drawn away from the Light and the peculiar custom of the faith."[26] Thus, education came to serve a sectarian purpose. Specifically, Quaker schools aimed to strengthen the separate identity of Friends by providing a "guarded education." To that end, Philadelphia Quakers, in 1799, established a boarding school at Westtown in rural Chester County to remove them from the worldly influences of the city and propagate the Quaker faith.[27]

Instead, the spiritual reformers reinvigorated the drive to abolish slavery within PYM. These Quaker abolitionists believed that slaveholding was a sinful practice that had caused the suffering and hardship of war and that PYM had to rid itself of the sinful practice to purify their religious body. The reformers also realized that abolishing slavery within the Yearly Meeting would take many years because several ministers and elders were wealthy farmers who owned human chattel and merchants who profited financially from a lucrative slave trade and the provisioning of plantation colonies.[28]

Benjamin Lay (1682–1759) was the most radical of all Quaker abolitionists, both in his approach and appearance. A hunched-back dwarf with spindly legs and an unusually large head, Lay stood just 4 feet 9 inches in height and sported a flowing white beard. He resorted to outrageous behavior to convince Quakers of the inconsistency of slaveholding and the Society of Friends belief in the spiritual equality of all human beings. Lay was especially accusatory of those leaders of Philadelphia Yearly Meeting, who were the richest and most powerful merchants in the colony and whose wealth came from owning and importing African slaves.[29]

Lay's most shocking ploy occurred in September 1738 at PYM, which met that year in a hexagonal structure in Burlington, New Jersey. After Friends entered the red-brick meetinghouse, took their seats, and settled into silent worship, the hunched-back dwarf marched into the building. Clad in a black cape and carrying a book that resembled a bible, Benjamin swaggered to the front of the room and plopped down on the facing bench. Concealed beneath his cloak was a soldier's uniform, complete with sword. The "bible" he held in his hands was hollow and inside was a container of red berry juice.

After a few moments, Lay sprang to his feet and began criticizing the wealthy Quakers for owning slaves. "All you slave masters who hold your fellow man in bondage, you violate every principle of our faith," he cried. "How can you call yourselves 'Quakers' when you don't respect our belief in the equality of all people? You might as well throw off the cloak and reveal your hypocrisy!" Unfastening the button of his long coat, Lay flung the garment to the floor exposing his soldier's uniform. The sight of the spectacle startled the peace-loving Quakers.

"God respects all colors of men equally, why don't you?" he demanded. "None of you would want to be a slave. Why not spare them and thrust a sword through their hearts as I do through this book!"

Friends became hysterical at the sight of the eccentric dwarf raising his sword in the air. With the force of a mighty hammer, Lay stabbed the book and red berry juice sprayed all over those seated near him. One of the elders, infuriated by his antics, vaulted off the facing bench, grabbed the Quaker dwarf by the arm, and ushered him out the door. "Friend, thee has said quite enough this morning!" Shortly after, Benjamin was disowned from the Society of Friends for his infamous "bladder of blood" charade.[30]

Ironically, Lay had not always viewed slavery as a heinous evil. In the 1720s, he himself owned slaves and used them to operate a dry goods store in the West Indies. Once, when he caught two slaves stealing merchandise, Lay nearly beat them to death. Troubled by his actions, Lay freed his slaves and vowed to abolish the unconscionable institution.[31] When other slave owners threatened his life unless he left the West Indies, the Quaker dwarf, in 1732, relocated to Philadelphia, eventually settling in the small village of Abington in present-day Montgomery County.[32]

Taking up residence in a small stone cottage that resembled a cave, Lay, in his mid-fifties, refused to eat food or wear clothing procured by slave labor. Instead, he cultivated a vegetable garden and fruit trees and spun his own wool for clothing.[33] He also devoted much time to meditation, reading books from his 200-volume library, and writing pamphlets against slavery.[34] But he was best known for the outrageous manner in which he protested human bondage.

An impatient man, Lay believed that words were meaningless unless they were accompanied by shocking actions to prove a point. Thus, he stunned Quaker slaveholders by directly confronting them with their hypocrisy. He could be just as intolerable to his Quaker neighbors, many of whom were farmers who used slave labor to cultivate their fields. One wintry Sunday, the dwarf stood outside the Abington Friends meetinghouse with one bare foot buried deep in a snowdrift.

"Oh, Benjamin," exclaimed a concerned Quaker matron as she approached the meetinghouse, "thee must remove thy foot or thee will get frostbite."

"You pretend compassion for me," he snapped. "Yet you do not feel for your slaves who are half-clad!"

Shocked by the insolent remark, the lady abruptly turned and trudged away.[35]

On another occasion, Lay, who had a great fondness for youngsters, kidnapped the child of a slave-holding neighbor to register the evils of slavery. He invited the youngster into his stone cottage and entertained him for several hours. Toward evening, the child's mother began to worry. "Benjamin, has thee seen my son?" she asked. "He was due home from school several hours ago and has not yet returned."

"You must be very concerned," Lay replied, pretending ignorance.

"It's just not like him to wander off like this, I cannot understand it."

"Do you think someone may have kidnapped him?" he suggested.

The mother became frantic. "Please, Benjamin," she sobbed. "Will thee help me find him?"

Satisfied by her anguish, Lay returned the child. Before they parted ways, though, he posed a question that would haunt her for many days:

"How do you think those poor slave mothers feel when their children are torn from them, never to be seen again?" A week later, the family freed their slaves.[36]

While many Quakers ignored Lay's outrageous actions, others began to consider the altruistic spirit in which he acted. His message was simple: "Do unto others as you would have them do to you." Nor were his efforts in vain. Benjamin Lay represented the most radical impulse of Quaker abolitionism, one that placed a single-minded commitment to eradicating slavery at any cost above the practical necessity of achieving that cause through society's established institutions.

John Woolman (1720–1772) was less dramatic than Lay, but every bit as passionate. He was a Quaker abolitionist from Mount Holly, New Jersey, 30 miles east of Philadelphia. Widely considered to be the primary figure of eighteenth-century Quaker faith and social reform, Woolman kept a journal of his anti-slavery activities in which tells of his struggles to follow the leading of the Inward Light his abhorrence of slavery and his desire to answer that of God in the less fortunate; a commitment he made very early in his life.[37]

As a youngster, Woolman discovered a robin's nest with several baby birds. He began throwing rocks at the mother robin to see if he could hit her. After killing the mother, the youngster felt great remorse, realizing that the babies had no chance of survival without her. Removing the nest from the tree, Woolman killed all the baby robins, believing it to be the most merciful thing to do. The experience weighed heavily and inspired him to love and protect all living things in the future.[38]

When he was in his early twenties, Woolman worked as a clerk for a merchant who asked him to write a bill of sale for a slave. Although he told his employer that he thought slaveholding was inconsistent with Christianity, he wrote the bill of sale. Shortly after, Woolman struck out on his own, becoming an independent and successful tradesman. He also refused to write bills of sale for slaves or wills that transferred the ownership of a slave to an heir.[39] Woolman eventually retired from business because he viewed profit-making as distracting from his Quaker faith. Instead, he began an itinerant ministry to preach against the evils of slavery.

Unlike Benjamin Lay, who used guerilla theater to shame Quaker slaveholders into freeing their chattel, Woolman worked within the Friends' tradition of seeking divine guidance and patiently waiting for Quakers to act on his concern about slaveholding. He also practiced what he preached. Woolman often accepted hospitality from a Quaker slaveholder when he traveled but insisted on paying the slaves for their work in attending to him. Similarly, he refused to use or eat any products procured by slave labor.

In 1754, Woolman published *Some Considerations on the Keeping of Negroes*, a pamphlet that aroused the moral conscience of PYM. Appealing to the Christian sympathies of his readers, Woolman reminded Quakers that slavery was a "contradiction to true religion itself," but that one should "exercise loving-kindness towards all men," including the slaveholder, in order to enjoy the "blessing of God." By focusing on the temporal as well as spiritual welfare of the slaveholder, rather than the dehumanization of the slave, Woolman encouraged Quakers to reconsider their involvement in the slave trade as well as the practice of slaveholding.[40]

The anti-slavery efforts of Benjamin Lay and John Woolman led PYM, in 1754, to declare its "uneasiness with the importation and purchasing of Negro slaves," stating that these practices were "not consistent with either Christianity or common justice." Instead of disowning those Friends who engaged in the slave trade, however, the Yearly Meeting urged them to reconsider "the case of the Africans" and how Friends would "feel if they were in their circumstances."[42] Four years later, PYM directed its constituent monthly meetings to "eliminate from membership all those who continued to buy or sell slaves."[43] However, enforcement of the 1758 discipline varied widely among the Quaker monthly meetings of southeastern Pennsylvania, ranging from disownment to lenient treatment for those who claimed ignorance of the change in discipline and promised to treat their slaves well in the future.[44]

The final step of ridding Philadelphia Yearly Meeting of slavery was left to Anthony Benezet (1713–1784), a Quaker educator, who devoted his life to the abolitionism and the emancipation and education of African Americans. Benezet, a French immigrant, arrived in Philadelphia in 1731. Attracted by the Quaker sympathy for human suffering, he left the Huguenot region to join the Society of Friends.[45] He taught at the Friends Public School at Fourth and Chestnut streets during the day and, in 1750, opened his home at night to tutor free blacks and slaves. Counter to the Friends Public School's focus on a classical education, Benezet, in his school, emphasized a return to basic literacy and moral instruction. He also broke with the FPS's focus on rote memorization and cultivated critical thinking among his students, believing that the pedagogy was more reflective of their natural intelligence.[46]

Like the other spiritual reformers in PYM, Benezet published many anti-slavery tracts including *A Caution to Great Britain and her Colonies, in a Short Representation of the Calamitous State of the Enslaved Negroes in the British Dominion* (1767) and *Some Historical Account of Guinea, with an Inquiry into the Rise and Progress of the Slave Trade* (1772). After many years of teaching at the Friends Public School and tutoring free blacks and slaves in the evening at his home on Chestnut Street, Benezet,

Anthony Benezet (1713–1784) established a school for children of color and founded one of the world's first abolitionist societies. He was a powerful force in the spiritual reformation of Philadelphia Yearly Meeting in the 1750s. Engraving by John W. Barber, New Haven, CT, 1850. (*Public Domain*)

in 1770, raised the money, built a structure, hired a teacher, and opened an African School specifically for this purpose. At a time when blacks were considered ignorant and incapable of formal training, Benezet's success in teaching them how to read, write, and to do simple arithmetic challenged the deeply rooted belief in black inferiority.[47]

However, Benezet's ultimate contribution to the abolitionist cause came on April 14, 1775 when he met with seven other Quakers and two non-Friends at the Rising Sun Tavern on Second Street to organize the "Society for the Relief of Free Negroes Unlawfully Held in Bondage," the first anti-slavery society in America. During the next few years, the group increased to twenty-four members, mostly Quaker artisans and merchants. They focused on intervention in the cases of African and Native Americans who claimed to have been illegally enslaved. Reorganized in February 1784 as the "Pennsylvania Abolition Society," the group remained a largely Quaker organization. Although they were still occupied with litigation on behalf of blacks who were illegally enslaved under existing laws, the organization began to place a stronger emphasis on the abolition of slavery itself.[48]

Benezet's activities and the constant lobbying of other Quaker reformers convinced PYM that slavery was a moral and spiritual evil that must be purged from their religious body. In 1776, PYM adopted a policy of disownment for slaveholding among members, setting a precedent for all the other yearly meetings in the United States.[49] What had begun a century earlier as a moral protest by a small group of Germantown Quakers had become a matter of spiritual integrity for the Society of Friends itself. Once this decisive step was taken, however, abolitionism was not as pressing a concern for the Society of Friends as it had been earlier.

Having abolished slavery within its ranks, PYM did not feel compelled to accept blacks into membership. While Friends welcomed them to attend their worship services, blacks were required to sit in special sections reserved for them, and only a tiny number were received into formal membership. Their reluctance was due to a fear of miscegenation, or marriage between the white and black races.[50] Nor did the majority of Philadelphia Quakers involve themselves in the larger campaign to abolish slavery across the nation.[51] That task was left to a small, radical minority of Friends, who would prevail in the nineteenth century.

Racist caricature mocking the pretentiousness and bigotry of Philadelphia Quakers toward their "social inferiors." In front of the open picket fence, a dark-skinned traveler, possibly an Irishman or African American, with buck teeth and carrying a knapsack, asks a rotund white Quaker man and his attractive prim daughter, "I say, this isn't the road to Philadelphy, honey, is it?" The father responds indignantly to the "Friend" that he is not only asking a question, but also telling a lie. Created by Edward W. Clay, Philadelphia, *c.* 1830. (*Library Company of Philadelphia*)

4

Speaking Truth to Power

After the American Revolution, Philadelphia took center stage in the political development of the new nation. Not only did the city host the convention which framed the federal constitution in 1787, it also became the seat of the national government for a decade when Congress relocated from New York City in 1790. Philadelphia also assumed a more dignified appearance befitting a capital city. Stretching nine blocks north to south along the Delaware River and just beyond the State House to the west, the city's walkways were lined with rows of buttonwood, willow, and poplar trees. Georgian-style buildings of the colonial era were dwarfed by new Classical edifices with free-standing marble columns like the First Bank of the United States, First Presbyterian Church, Merchants' Exchange, and Second Bank of the United States.[1]

A steady influx of English, German, and Scots-Irish immigrants swelled the city's population from 30,000 on the eve of the Revolution to just over 164,000 in 1830.[2] Philadelphia was home to Quakers, Lutherans, Catholics, Jews, Methodists, Moravians, Baptists, Presbyterians, Episcopalians, and others. Gentry and wealthy merchants lived in the nearby countryside, while the middle-class resided in the red-brick townhouses that spanned the city. Tradesmen lived in and sold their wares from more modest row homes off Market Street, while free blacks and white laborers who made up the industrious poor resided in the least desirable dwellings along the Delaware waterfront, or outside the city limits.[3] Economic survival was a difficult challenge for these groups. Disadvantaged by little or no education and limited job training, the underprivileged accounted for 32 percent of all convictions in the mayor's court.[4] Their circumstances worsened in 1793 with the outbreak of the dreaded Yellow Fever epidemic. With inadequate housing, insufficient diets, and no healthcare, the lower classes were most vulnerable to the fever which claimed the lives of approximately 5,000 of the city's 45,000 residents.[5]

By the end of the eighteenth century, Quakers were in the minority. Many members had been disowned for slaveholding or supporting the Revolutionary War. Others left the faith voluntarily to join other denominations, especially the Episcopalian, Presbyterian, and Methodist churches. Still others were attracted to the social amenities the city had to offer and PYM discouraged, including theater, music, and art. At the same time, those who remained in the Quaker fold became more committed to their faith and to the benevolent reform it encouraged.[6]

Between 1790 and 1850, the city's Quakers initiated a plethora of reforms that reached a zenith in the nineteenth century. Prison reform, care of the mentally ill, common schooling, Native American and women's rights, and especially the abolition of slavery were all championed by Quakers, though other religious groups were also involved and even took the lead. In this way, Friends proved themselves to be loyal citizens of the young nation and to silence public criticism of their refusal to fight in the War for Independence.[7] Their humanitarian efforts were acknowledged by President George Washington. "Your principles and conduct are well known to me," Washington wrote to Philadelphia Yearly Meeting shortly after he assumed executive office, "and it is doing the people called Quakers no more than justice to say that except for their declining to share with others the burden of the common defense [during the Revolutionary War] there is no denomination among us who are more exemplary and useful citizens."[8]

The Quakers' reputation as pioneers of social reform is grounded in a belief of "speaking truth to power," or using truth and a non-violent approach to oppose acts of oppression by the government or any civil authority that has the power to punish human beings in some way. "Speaking truth" is the "outward" expression of an "inward" spiritual experience for Quakers, which inspires them to act. Friends believe that that inward experience comes not only from the divine, but from the heart, from a place of faith, and a place of love. When that inward truth is spoken "to power," Friends are exercising the courage to speak—and act on—that truth to those in positions of authority who may not want to hear it but have the authority to punish them for speaking it. Thus, "speaking truth to power" is an expression of both faithfulness and courage and one that has inspired Friends historically to reform society to bring all of God's creatures closer to the Almighty.[9]

The Quaker concern for the poor is a fine example of this principle. Friends, as early as 1713, established an Almshouse which offered food, housing, and basic healthcare for the indigent, and a workhouse to provide training and small menial jobs for the industrious poor. This was the first institution of its kind in America to care for the poor.[10] Friends also understood that there was a dangerous cycle between poverty and crime. If not addressed, the poor resorted to criminal activity to survive. Once incarcerated, there was no effort made to rehabilitate the offenders or offer them the training needed to secure employment upon their release. Thus, they would return to a life of poverty and crime. This understanding inspired the city's Quakers to involve themselves in prison reform.

Friends believed that all people are innately good and that even those who break the law are still human and should be respected as such. They were appalled by the crude practices and primitive living conditions they saw at Philadelphia's Walnut Street Prison, the city's principal jail. Regardless of age, gender, or crime, all offenders were incarcerated together in one large room: aged men with young women, physically infirm with criminally insane, condemned murderers with juvenile delinquents. Riots, frequent escapes, and overcrowding prevailed. Bedding was seldom provided, and there were no facilities for bathing. There was a high incidence of communicable disease. Inmates with money bribed the guards for favors, while the poor were reduced to begging from whoever might pass by the open but barred windows. Punishment included bodily mutilation, public whipping, and torture, all designed with the added purpose of evoking fear and respect for authority among the public.[11]

The Friends Almshouse, located on the south side of Walnut Street between 3rd and 4th Streets, Philadelphia, was intended to house destitute Quakers as well as poverty-stricken people of other denominations. Engraving by Thomas Sinclair, Philadelphia, 1840. (*Library of Congress*)

Quakers were shocked by these conditions and practices, believing they only encouraged even more crime and vice. In 1787, they joined with such prominent Philadelphians as statesman and inventor Benjamin Franklin, Dr. Benjamin Rush, a renowned physician and Bishop William White, rector of the Episcopalian Christ Church and founded the Philadelphia Society for Relieving Distressed Prisoners. Believing that their "obligations to humanity were not canceled by the crimes of their fellow creatures," the group set out to improve conditions in the city's prisons by rehabilitating criminals rather than punishing them by torture, dismemberment, and even death.[12] To this end, they reopened Walnut Street Jail as a state penitentiary in 1790. For the first time, inmates were required to wear uniforms to discourage escape attempts. Work opportunities were made available as a means of coping with lengthy prison sentences and to reimburse the state for prison costs. Sixteen individual cells were designed to prevent communication between inmates. Convicts were permitted to read, but only religious literature. They were encouraged to reflect on their transgressions while spending most of their day in their cells—a concept known as "penitence."[13]

The penitentiary concept was drawn from Quaker religious practices, stressing the value of silence to facilitate an inward communication with the divine and became the basis for the opening in 1829 of Eastern State Penitentiary and the widely adopted "Pennsylvania System" of prison management. Eastern State further developed the concept of rehabilitation through solitary confinement where prisoners were given the opportunity to meditate about their past sins and resolve to live a better life. This revolutionary concept of "penitence"—better known as the "Pennsylvania System"—embraced the twin notions of punishment and reform. In place of physical pain, the inmate would be punished by the loss of his freedom. Prisoners were hooded upon their entry and every effort was made to isolate them from human contact with the outside world during their stay.[14]

The original cellblocks radiated from a central rotunda, allowing for maximum efficiency of security, movement, and surveillance. Individual cells, each with a small exercise yard, were furnished with a bed, toilet, worktable, skylight, and Bible, reminding the prisoner that penitence would be achieved through the light from heaven, the word of God, and honest work. Although the penitentiary's radial design and the mission of rehabilitating the prisoner inspired the construction of 300 similar facilities around the world, the penitentiary concept was not widely adopted in the United States. It was considered too expensive. Instead, American prisons followed the congregate model established in Auburn, New York, where prisoners were confined in individual cells at night, but required to work together during the day.[15]

Designed by prominent Philadelphia architect John Haviland and opened on October 25, 1829, Eastern State was the world's first true penitentiary, a prison designed to inspire penitence in the hearts of prisoners. The building's seven cell blocks, radial floor plan, and system of solitary confinement was the model for over 300 prisons worldwide. Engraving by Peter S. Duval, Philadelphia, 1856. (*Library Company of Philadelphia*)

Related to prison reform for Philadelphia Friends was the care of the mentally ill. Early religious persecution resulted in the imprisonment of thousands of English Quakers, making them well-acquainted with the poor conditions of jails. Some of these early Friends were driven to the verge of insanity and were punished, baited, and exhibited for the amusement of the public.[16] Although Pennsylvania Hospital, established in 1751, was the first institution in the world to offer medical care for the insane, patients were kept in the cellar, and chained by the waist and ankle to cell walls. Therapy was also crude. Patients' scalps were shaved. They were bled almost to death and given enemas to exorcise their inner demons.[17]

In 1811, Thomas Scattergood proposed that Friends establish an "Asylum for the Relief of Persons Deprived of the Use of Their Reason." He reasoned that "if in every person there is some part of the divine, then insanity, like slavery and poverty, is an obstacle to be removed on the path to enlightenment and, like slavery and poverty, curable." Philadelphia Yearly Meeting acted on Scattergood's concern appointing a committee to raise funds and organize the construction of "Frankford Mental Asylum."[18] Scattergood was joined on the committee by Samuel Tuke, whose family established a similar institution for the mentally ill in England in 1796, and Isaac Bonsall, who would be the hospital's first superintendent.[19]

When Frankford Asylum opened in 1813, it was the first private mental hospital in the United States. Intended for the "suitable accommodation of persons who are deprived of the use of their reason," the Asylum provided patients with "requisite medical aid, [and] such tender, sympathetic attention as may soothe their agitated minds, and under the Divine Blessing, facilitate their recovery." Friends Hospital, as it is known today, operated on the principles of "occupation" and "nonrestraint." Patients who were able were given occupational therapy, which included working on the hospital grounds, taking rides through the surrounding park, playing tennis or croquet, and attending lectures. These practices were revolutionary in the nineteenth century but are standard in good private mental hospitals today.[20]

Philadelphia Quakers also played an instrumental role in founding a public school system to address the educational needs of the growing numbers of poor and idle children in the city. Although the Pennsylvania Legislature, in 1802, provided for the urban poor to be taught in private schools at public expense, the arrangement proved to be inadequate. Roberts Vaux (1786–1836), a prominent lawyer and overseer of the Friends Public School, felt a moral responsibility to find a solution to the problem. Vaux, who at one time was a member of more than fifty philanthropic societies, secured funding from the state government in the early 1810s to have the children of the poor taught in the several charity schools founded by Quakers. Established in 1818, this loose network of "public schools" was overseen by a board of controllers, chaired by Vaux, and taught the greatest number of children for the least cost by having brighter students teach other children under the supervision of an adult monitor.[21]

Within a decade's time, Vaux realized that something more was needed. In 1827, he, along with several other Quaker and non-Quaker reformers, established the Pennsylvania Society for the Promotion of Public Schools, which lobbied the state legislature to create schools that would be tuition free and open to all children. His vision became a reality through the Free Schools Acts of 1834 and 1835 and the Consolidation Act of 1836, which opened Philadelphia's public schools to all school-age children.[22]

These public schools grew so quickly that they enrolled 17,000 students within two years. To manage such numbers, the board of controllers

Right: Thomas Scattergood (1784–1814) believed in the moral treatment of mentally ill patients and was instrumental in the founding of the Friends Asylum for the Insane, the first mental hospital in the United States to follow this model. (*Quaker Collection, Haverford College Library, Haverford, PA*)

Below: Friends Asylum for the Insane, founded in 1813, was the first private psychiatric hospital in the United States. Opened to patients in 1817, the institution stood on land that formerly was a 52-acre farm in Oxford Township, near Frankford, 6 miles northeast of Philadelphia. Engraving by George Lehman, Philadelphia, 1836. (*Library of Congress*)

Quaker philanthropist Roberts Vaux (1786–1836) was an Overseer of the Friends Public School who helped establish Philadelphia's public school system. Engraving by Peter S. Duval, Philadelphia, *c.* 1840. (*Library Company of Philadelphia*)

divided students into three ability groups. In October 1838, they also opened Central High School for Boys to prepare youngsters for employment in the city's growing business industry. With these achievements, Philadelphia joined the common school movement that institutionalized and standardized the way most children were educated.[23]

While Philadelphia Quakers championed many institutional reforms, they also promoted the rights of minorities. Native Americans were one of those groups. Pressured by white frontiersmen and the United States government, which encouraged western settlement, Indians were being displaced from their lands west of the Appalachian Mountains. In 1793, two Iroquois messengers traveled from the Northwest Territory to Philadelphia to request that Quakers attend a council at Sandusky, Ohio, between the U.S. government and the Six Nations. In response, the Philadelphia Yearly Meeting sent a delegation of six members. Although the council did not settle the differences between the federal government and the Iroquois, it did convince the Yearly Meeting to establish, in 1796, an Indian Affairs Committee that mediated between the federal government and Native Americans at later gatherings.[24] In subsequent years, this committee worked among the Senecas, teaching them farming skills and, in 1847, established a boarding school for their children so they could learn the ways of white society.[25]

Quakers also promoted women's rights. Because of their belief in the spiritual equality of men and women, Friends were more progressive than other Protestant denominations regarding female leadership within their religious body. Philadelphia Quakers established a separate yearly meeting for women shortly after the founding of Pennsylvania in 1682. This institutional body served as the vehicle for women to exercise leadership roles in the ministry, education, and philanthropy. Quaker women were engaged in the itinerant ministry, collected funds for their various reform involvements, established schools, promote the boycott of goods manufactured by slaves, and lobbied for emancipation.[26]

Despite the success of their many reform activities, early nineteenth-century Quakers were divided. In the 1820s, younger, city-dwelling Friends who were the more progressive-thinking members of PYM, came under the growing influence of a new, more vibrant evangelical movement. While these evangelical-oriented Quakers did not stress an emotional conversion experience like other evangelical groups, they accused the elder members of PYM of undervaluing the divinity of Christ and Scripture, which were, for them, the authoritative sources of divine revelation. These more progressive-thinking Quakers, many of whom belonged to the city's merchant class, became known as "Orthodox."

On the other hand, elder members of the Yearly Meeting, known as "Quietists," emphasized the role of the Inward Light in guiding individual faith and conscience, often in the meditative silence of the meeting for worship. They accused the Orthodox of abandoning traditional Quaker teachings on these subjects by relying on human will, reason, and intellect, which contaminated the experience of the Inward Light. As the 1820s unfolded, these rural, Quietist Friends became followers of Elias Hicks (1748–1839), a travelling Quaker minister from Long Island, New York, who championed a more spiritualistic and less dogmatic approach. Like Hicks, the rural Friends viewed the Inner Light, or indwelling Christ, as the unerring source of divine revelation and took the name "Hicksite."

The theological differences between these two groups represented the unraveling of a delicate synthesis of quietism, evangelism, and rationalism that existed from the very beginnings of Quakerism in the mid-seventeenth century and resulted in social, geographic, and generational divisions among nineteenth-century Friends. Nor was this conflict unique to Philadelphia Quakers. Congregationalists were dividing into Unitarians and Trinitarians, the Presbyterians into New School and Old School.[27]

The Quaker conflict came to a head in 1827 during a gathering of PYM when both factions tried to assert their rights to leadership. The Hicksites stormed out of Arch Street Meeting House and built their own meetinghouse on Race Street. About two-thirds of PYM's membership were Hicksites, while the remaining third comprised the Orthodox faction which retained the use of the Arch Street Meeting House. Now there were two Philadelphia Yearly Meetings, one Hicksite and one Orthodox, with each side refusing to recognize the legitimacy of the other.[28]

Elias Hicks (1748–1830), a traveling minister from Long Island, New York, considered obedience to the Inner Light to be the sole rule of the Quaker faith rather than Biblical revelation. This controversial view caused a major schism within Quakerism and one that bears his name. Engraving by Edward Hopper, New York, *c.* 1830. (*Library of Congress*)

The schism, better known as the "Great Separation," resulted in the division of monthly meetings and once jointly owned properties as well as the creation of separate schools for each faction. The Orthodox retained control of the Westtown Boarding school, founded in 1799 in Chester County, and established two colleges outside the city: Haverford College for young men (1833) and Bryn Mawr College (1885) for young women. Desiring the opportunity for a higher education of their members, the Hicksites founded coeducational Swarthmore College in 1864, in Delaware County, and George School, a co-educational boarding school, in 1893 in Bucks County.[29]

The schism also had a profound impact on Quaker benevolence. While the Orthodox encouraged involvement with non-Quakers in various reform activities, the Hicksites tended to work strictly among Friends. In the 1850s, even this group divided over the issue of how vigorously abolition and women's rights should be pursued and whether to join with non-Friends in either reform activity. As a result, the Pennsylvania Yearly Meeting of Progressive Friends, which welcomed non-Quaker reformers, broke away from the Hicksite Yearly Meeting and built their own meetinghouse at Longwood, Chester County.[30]

The Great Separation revealed the stark differences among Quakers over anti-slavery activity. Although PYM abandoned its concern for the peculiar institution of slavery after 1776 when it made slaveholding a cause for disownment, individual Quakers picked up the fallen standard, becoming involved in the larger movement to abolish slavery in American society. These anti-slavery Friends joined the Pennsylvania Abolition Society to lobby the state legislature for their cause, which resulted in the passage of the Gradual Abolition Act of 1780. According to the measure, "all slaves were to be registered" and "every Negro and Mulatto child born within the state [of] [Pennsylvania] after the passage of the act on March 1, 1780 [would] be freed upon reaching the age of twenty-eight." When released, those slaves would "receive the same freedom dues and other privileges as an indentured servant."[31] The act also prohibited Pennsylvanians from importing slaves, though they could still purchase and sell those slaves who had been registered under the measure. At the same time, the law condemned those slaves born prior to March 1, 1780 to a lifetime of bondage extending the duration of the peculiar institution in the Keystone State until 1847.[32]

Nevertheless, slavery gradually declined in Pennsylvania after 1780. In addition to those slaves freed under the act upon turning twenty-eight years old, there were those owners who provided for the manumission of slaves in their wills, and others during their lifetimes. Accelerating the process was the Pennsylvania Anti-Slavery Society, a more proactive group than the Pennsylvania Abolition Society, which purchased many slaves and promptly set them free. Still other slaves escaped bondage by running away. Thus, between 1790 and 1800, the number of slaves in Pennsylvania declined from 3,737 to 1,706, and by 1810 to 795. In 1840, there were just sixty-four slaves remaining in the state, and by 1850, there were none.[33] The reason for this gradual, two-generation process was to avoid an abrupt halt to slavery to limit the financial loss to the state's slaveholders.

Philadelphia witnessed a similar decline in the slave population, but it coincided with an increase in the free black population consisting of native-born slaves as well as runaways. Between 1790 and 1800, for example, the city's slave population decreased from 301 to fifty-five, as the number of free blacks grew from 1,849 to 6,028 in the same period. In 1810, there were just two slaves remaining in Philadelphia and that number dropped to none in 1840, while the free black population almost doubled during that same span from nearly 10,000 in 1810 to about 18,000 in 1840.[34] Quaker efforts figured prominently in both the decline of slavery and the growth of the free black community in the city.

What is important to note, however, is that not all Quakers were abolitionists—only a small minority—and those who were abolitionists were divided on how to achieve emancipation. There were significant differences in approach. Some Quaker abolitionists refused to work with non-Quaker abolitionists, preferring to appeal to the moral conscience of slaveholders by refusing to purchase goods procured by slave labor. Other Friends joined non-Quakers in establishing anti-slavery organizations, which raised funds for the cause and elevated public awareness through the publication of newspapers and pamphlets.[35] One of these was the American Anti-Slavery Society co-founded by Lucretia Mott in Philadelphia in 1833. Seeking immediate emancipation, this interdenominational organization's more than 850 local auxiliaries in fifteen states forwarded more than 400,000 antislavery petitions with nearly one million signatures to Congress by 1838.[36] Still other Philadelphia Quakers lobbied state and federal governments to adopt anti-slavery legislation.

There were also differences in the timetable for emancipation. There were those Friends who advocated a gradual approach followed by the relocation, or colonization, of former slaves in Africa. These Quakers were called "gradualists." There were others who demanded immediate emancipation and the amalgamation, or complete integration, of former slaves into white mainstream society. Accordingly, these more radical Friends were called "immediatists." Still other Quaker abolitionists held positions that ran the gamut between these two extremes.[37]

The most radical—and smallest—group of anti-slavery Friends were those who violated federal law by participating in the Underground Railroad, the clandestine and illegal movement of African American slaves escaping out of the South to a loosely organized network of abolitionists who assisted them to freedom in the North. Quaker Underground Railroad agents broke with Philadelphia Yearly Meeting in the 1840s and established their own "Pennsylvania Yearly Meeting of Progressive Friends" at Longwood in rural Chester County in 1853. Revolting against the rural monthly meetings, which were more conservative on matters of religious doctrine and humanitarian reform, Progressive Friends were more concerned about reform than religion. Thus, all people were invited to join the Longwood Progressive Friends Meeting, without regard to sex, race, or religious denomination, and their reform involvements ran the gamut from abolitionism to prison reform, and temperance to common schooling. But no reform was as important than the abolition of slavery.[38]

Believing that God's law superseded civil law, many members rejected the federal Fugitive Slave Law of 1850 requiring every citizen to aid in the recapture of runaway slaves or face a fine and/or imprisonment. Thomas Whitson stated the group's philosophy when he declared that the "popular notion that government must be obeyed, whatever its requirements, was all wrong." "Divine Law," Whitson insisted was "superior to acts of Congress," especially if it meant "destroying unjust measures."[39]

"Reformers ought to be satisfied to be destructives," echoed Lucretia Mott, Philadelphia's most prominent Quaker female reformer. "If we are

William Penn (1644–1718). Quaker founder of Pennsylvania in old age. Sketch by Frances Place. (*Historical Society of Pennsylvania, Philadelphia, PA*)

Hannah Callowhill Penn (1671–1726). Penn's second wife served as acting proprietor of Pennsylvania from 1712, after her husband suffered a series of strokes, until her death in 1726. Sketch by Frances Place. (*Historical Society of Pennsylvania, Philadelphia, PA*)

William Penn's Treaty with the Indians. Painting by Benjamin West, *c.* 1771–1772. West's painting depicts the legendary meeting between William Penn and members of the Lenni Lenape tribe at Shackamaxon on the Delaware River. By depicting the three factions that shaped Pennsylvania for most of the eighteenth century—Native Americans, Quakers, and merchants—united in the act of settlement, West created a powerful symbol of peace. Although the scene is allegorical rather than historical, the image has become an icon of American history. (*Pennsylvania Academy of the Fine Arts, Philadelphia, PA*)

Pennsbury Manor was the 8,000-acre Bucks County estate of William Penn, who desired "a country life for [his] children." Located about 25 miles north of Philadelphia along the Delaware River, Pennsbury was home to the Penn family from 1699 to 1701. Today, the site is administered by the Pennsylvania Historical and Museum Commission and is open year-round to the public for tours. (*Author*)

Thomas Penn (1702–1775). The son of William Penn and chief proprietor of Pennsylvania from 1746 to 1775, Thomas Penn negotiated the infamous Walking Purchase with the Lenape Indians, cheating them out of 1,200,000 acres of their tribal lands. Painting by Arthur Davis, *c.* 1752. (*Public Domain*)

Benjamin Lay (1682–1759). Lay, an Anglo-American abolitionist, was a hunchback dwarf with a protruding chest, and his arms were as long as his legs. His early and dramatic anti-slavery protests culminated in the abolition of the slave trade among Quakers. Painting by William Williams, 1791. (*National Portrait Gallery, Washington, D.C.*)

In September 1738, Burlington Friends Meeting House was the scene of Benjamin Lay's most infamous anti-slavery protests. Known as the "Bladder of Blood" stunt, Lay plunged a sword into an animal bladder containing pokeberry juice and the mock "blood" splattered over the slaveholding Quaker elders at the gathering. Facsimile painting by J. Collins, 1900, after original painted by Jefferson Gauntt, 1833. (*Quaker Collection, Haverford College Library, Haverford, Pennsylvania*)

The Free Quaker Meeting House, located on the corner of 5th and Arch Streets in Philadelphia, was established in 1781 as the place of worship for those Friends who supported the American Revolution and were disowned by Philadelphia Yearly Meeting for doing so. Today the Meeting House is part of Independence National Historical Park and is open to the public. (*Author*)

Right: Lucretia Mott (1793–1880). Founder of the Philadelphia Female Anti-Slavery Society, Mott was the city's most prominent female reformer. Photograph by F. Gutekunst, Philadelphia, PA *c.* 1870–1880. (*Friends Historical Library, Swarthmore College, Swarthmore, Pennsylvania*)

Below: Executive Committee of the Pennsylvania Anti-Slavery Society. Founded in 1838, the Pennsylvania Anti-Slavery Society welcomed men, women, and black people into membership. Pictured here is the executive committee, which included Lucretia Mott, who is seated next to her husband James at the right-hand side of the front row. Seated to Lucretia's right is the free black abolitionist Robert Purvis, also a founder of the American Abolition Society and president of the Pennsylvania Anti-Slavery Society from 1845 to 1850. (*Friends Historical Library, Swarthmore College, Swarthmore, Pennsylvania*)

Left: Quaker merchant Thomas Garrett (1789–1871) was a station master on the Underground Railroad in Wilmington, Delaware, who channeled fugitive slaves across the Chester County, Pennsylvania, border to Philadelphia. (*Chester County History Center, West Chester, PA*)

Below: Built in 1854, the Progressive Friends Meeting House was a beacon of Antebellum reform, where members discussed slavery, women's rights, capital punishment, prison reform, and other issues. Speakers included Frederick Douglass, Sojourner Truth, Harriet Beecher Stowe, Susan B. Anthony, William Lloyd Garrison, and Lucretia Mott. Located at 300 Greenwood Road, Kennett Square, PA, the building serves as the Chester County Visitors' Center. (*Chester County History Center, West Chester, PA*)

Passmore Williamson (1822–1895), a Quaker abolitionist, was served with a writ of *habeas corpus* by federal U.S. District Court John K. Kane under the Fugitive Slave Law of 1850 to produce Jane Johnson and her two sons in court. Since Williamson did not actually know where they were held and could not provide information of their whereabouts, Judge Kane charged him with contempt of court and sentenced him to ninety days in Philadelphia's Moyamensing Prison. Williamson's incarceration dramatically expanded news coverage of the case and generated a national debate about the extension of "Slave Power" over state law, as Pennsylvania did not recognize slavery. (*Chester County History Center, West Chester, PA*)

Norwood Penrose Hallowell (1836–1914) attended Haverford College before enlisting in the Union Army. One of three Philadelphia Quaker brothers who served with distinction during the Civil War, Hallowell, in 1862, was promoted to captain of the 20th Massachusetts Volunteer Infantry and was wounded at the Battle of Antietam. In April 1863, he was made second-in-command to Colonel Robert Gould Shaw of the 54th Massachusetts, one of the first all-black regiments in the Union Army. A month later, Hallowell was given command of his own all-black regiment, the 55th Massachusetts Infantry. *Carte de visite* by Broadbent & Co., 1862. (*Quaker Collection, Haverford College, Haverford, PA*)

Eliza P. Gurney (1801–1881) visited President Lincoln in October 1862 and assured him of Quaker support in his efforts to end slavery and the Civil War. She then prayed with him. Lincoln was so moved that he maintained a correspondence with her. When Lincoln was assassinated, one of Eliza's letters that had been carefully "treasured up" by him was in his breast pocket when the fatal shot struck him. (*Quaker Collection, Haverford College Library, Haverford, PA*)

Joseph Wharton (1826–1909) was a Philadelphia Quaker industrialist. He was involved in mining, manufacturing, and education. He founded the Wharton School at the University of Pennsylvania, co-founded the Bethlehem Steel company, and was one of the founders of Swarthmore College. Photo taken in 1850 by unknown photographer. (*Public Domain*)

Superintendent Asa C. Tuttle (pictured in top row at center) with Quaker teachers and students at Modoc School, Indian Territory, Oklahoma, in 1872. (*Quaker Collection, Haverford College, Haverford, PA*)

Opposite: The William Penn statue, sculpted by Alexander Milne Calder, stands atop Philadelphia's City Hall. It is 36 feet, 8 inches tall and weighs 26 tons. Cast in bronze by the Tacony Iron and Metal Works in 1892, the statue was displayed in the courtyard for two years before being raised to the top of the edifice. (*Public Domain*)

Above: The Quaker-founded American Friends Service Committee fed hungry school children in post-World War I Germany. Eventually AFSC was chartered by President Herbert Hoover to provide the United States-sponsored relief to all needy Germans. (*American Friends Service Committee Collection, Swarthmore College, Swarthmore, PA*)

Left: Henry Cadbury (1883–1974), a Quaker historian and writer, was one of the founders of the American Friends Service Committee. Thrifty by nature, Cadbury, in 1947, had to borrow a tuxedo to accept the 1947 Nobel Peace Prize in Oslo, Norway. (*Quaker Collection, Haverford College, Haverford, PA*)

One of the most influential Quakers of the twentieth century, Rufus Jones (1863–1948) was a historian, theologian, writer, and philosopher. He was also instrumental in the establishment of the Haverford Emergency Unit, a precursor to the American Friends Service Committee. (*Lower Merion Historical Society, Bala Cynwyd, PA*)

Bayard Rustin (1912–1987), an African American Quaker, was a mentor to the Civil Rights leader, the Rev. Dr. Martin Luther King, Jr., He is pictured here speaking to youngsters before a peace demonstration in the late 1960s. (*Library of Congress*)

William Penn Charter School, founded in 1689 as the Friends Public School, is the oldest Quaker school in the nation. (*William Penn Charter School*)

Westtown School was founded in 1799 as a coeducational boarding school by Philadelphia Yearly Meeting to provide to a guarded education for the city's Quaker children. Today, Westtown is the oldest, continuously operating coeducational boarding school in the country. (*Westtown School, West Chester, PA*)

Designed by Owen Biddle, Jr., Arch Street Meeting House was built between 1804 and 1811 on property deeded by William Penn as a burial ground for Friends. Today, the Meeting House is a National Historic Landmark and serves as home to Philadelphia Yearly Meeting of the Religious Society of Friends. (*Arch Street Meeting House, Philadelphia, PA*)

The interior of Arch Street Meeting House is an example of the Georgian architectural style, and it incorporates the Quaker ideals of simplicity, plainness, and equality. The two-story wood-frame building consists of a large first-floor meeting space with benches, and an interior second-story gallery. Since worship involves silent contemplation without clergy or ritual, there is no need for an altar, pulpit, or other religious symbols. (*Arch Street Meeting House, Philadelphia, PA*)

to be 'sharp threshing instruments having teeth we should have some other name than 'reformers.'"[40]

The Longwood Meeting House was often a gathering site for prominent abolitionists, who traveled from all over the country to speak there. Consistent with the Progressive Friends' insistence on a free exchange of ideas, no abolitionist was denied the opportunity to speak. William Lloyd Garrison, the editor of anti-slavery newspaper *The Liberator*, and famed black orator Frederick Douglass, for example, were frequent speakers at Longwood, despite their celebrated conflict over the extent of black leadership in abolitionist reform and the moral efficacy of participating in politics in a country where slavery was legal.[41]

Progressive Friends also established a network of safe houses for fugitives and channeled them to conductors along the Underground Railroad's Eastern Line, which ran from Maryland and Delaware through central and southeastern Pennsylvania and ultimately to Canada. One stationmaster, Thomas Garrett, a Quaker merchant of Wilmington, Delaware, claimed to have assisted 2,700 runaways—including Harriet Tubman—in his three decades as an Underground Railroad agent.[42] Garrett channeled most of his runaways to William Still, a free black abolitionist in Philadelphia who served as the clerk of the Pennsylvania Anti-Slavery Society's Vigilance Committee. Still coordinated the movement of freedom seekers on the Eastern Line communicating with "station masters" and "conductors" across the eastern seaboard and into Canada. Not only did he assist some 995 fugitives who came under his care between 1853 and 1861, but he interviewed each one in the hope of reuniting them with enslaved family members when slavery ended. Still's interviews formed the basis of an 800-page book he published in 1872 titled *The Underground Railroad*.[43]

Passmore Williamson was another Philadelphia Quaker abolitionist who worked closely with William Still. He was imprisoned for his involvement in the daring escape of Jane Johnson, a house servant of Colonel John H. Wheeler. Wheeler, a North Carolina slaveholder, was appointed U.S. ambassador to Nicaragua in 1855. On July 18, he was passing through Philadelphia *en route* to New York where he would embark for Central America. With him were Johnson and her two young sons. When Still learned of their arrival and of Jane's desire for freedom, he met them at the city's docks with Williamson, a member of the Philadelphia Vigilance Committee.

As the two abolitionists confronted Wheeler and advised Johnson that she was free to go, a crowd gathered. When Williamson informed the colonel that Pennsylvania law did not recognize the property rights of slaveholders, and that Johnson had the right to declare her freedom if she chose, Wheeler became enraged and had to be restrained by five black

Quaker abolitionist Thomas Garrett (1789–1871) was a leader in the Underground Railroad movement. He assisted 2,700 African American slaves to freedom. For his efforts, Garrett was threatened, harassed, and assaulted. A $10,000 bounty was established for his capture. Engraving by T. Ellwood Zell, Philadelphia, *c.* 1870 in William Still, *Underground Railroad* (1872), p. 647. (*Public Domain*)

William Still (1821–1902) was a free black abolitionist and chairman of the Pennsylvania Anti-Slavery Society's General Vigilance Committee. He coordinated the Eastern Line of the Underground Railroad from Delaware to Canada with the assistance of other Quaker abolitionists. Engraving by T. Ellwood Zell, Philadelphia, *c.* 1870 in William Still, *Underground Railroad* (1872), p. ii. (*Public Domain*)

bystanders. Meanwhile Still escorted Johnson and her sons to a waiting coach and transported them to his home.[44]

Still and the five black deckhands were later charged with forcible abduction, riot, and assault by Wheeler. The charges against Williamson were more complicated. Under petition by Wheeler, U.S. District Court Justice John K. Kane, a pro-slavery judge, issued a writ of *habeas corpus* to Williamson to produce Johnson and her two sons in court. When Williamson told Kane that he literally did not know her whereabouts as Still never informed him where he took Johnson, the judge charged him with contempt of court for not producing the slave. In addition, Kane charged Williamson with violating the Fugitive Slave Law of 1850, which required even citizens of free states to cooperate in returning fugitives to their owners. As a result, the Quaker abolitionist was sentenced to three months in Moyamensing Prison.[45]

On August 29, Still and the five black deckhands were tried on the charges brought by Wheeler. Although Johnson and her sons were living in New York, she returned for the trial. She caused a dramatic stir by testifying at length that Still had not abducted her, nor had any of the charged men forced her to go. Johnson also admitted that she had long planned to gain her freedom in the North during the trip, either in Philadelphia or New York. Her testimony refuted the prosecution and gained acquittal for Still and three of the deckhands, and reduced charges and sentences for the other two.[46]

Jane Johnson (*c.* 1820–1872), a black slave from North Carolina, gained her freedom in Philadelphia on July 18, 1855, with the assistance of William Still and Passmore Williamson. The escape challenged the 1850 Fugitive Slave Law and resulted in a precedent-setting legal case in nineteenth-century Pennsylvania. Engraving by T. Ellwood Zell, *c.* 1870 in William Still, *Underground Railroad* (1872), p. 80. (*Public Domain*)

Protected by state and local officials, Johnson was rushed out of the city, eluding federal marshals. She and her two sons remained free and later relocated to Boston, where she found work as a seamstress.

Williamson, on the other hand, remained incarcerated. He spent a total of 100 days—July 27 to November 3, 1855—inside Moyamensing Prison. During that time, his case attracted extensive press coverage and he received several hundred visitors, including prominent black abolitionists Frederick Douglass and Harriet Tubman.[47] Lucretia Mott noted that Williamson's imprisonment was extremely helpful to the abolitionist cause, and divulged that his father, Thomas, was "only afraid Passmore will come out of Prison too soon."[48]

Claiming that he was illegally imprisoned, Williamson, suffering from ill health, filed his own writ of *habeas corpus* with the Pennsylvania Supreme Court, but it was denied. Finally, on November 3, Kane, yielding to overwhelming public pressure, freed the Quaker abolitionist, who later sued the judge for illegal imprisonment.[49]

Passmore Williamson, Lucretia Mott, and Thomas Garrett, as well as the other members of the Progressive Friends Meeting, never officially sponsored the Underground Railroad, realizing that to do so would imperil their own lives as well as those they were attempting to aid.

Quaker participation in the abolitionist movement also served as a springboard to oppose gender inequality. Female Quaker abolitionists soon realized that they, like black slaves, were treated as property in a society dominated by men. Of all Philadelphia's Quaker reformers, Lucretia Mott (1793–1880), a diminutive, gentle person who became an outspoken force when defending her antislavery convictions, led the fight to gain greater recognition for women. Co-founder of the American Anti-Slavery Society with William Lloyd Garrison in 1833, Mott, known within abolitionists ranks as the "Black Man's Goddess," recruited most of the female membership of that body. Five years later, in 1838, she founded the Philadelphia Female Anti-Slavery Society, whose members included both white and black women.[50] Mott's activities were too progressive for the tastes of nineteenth-century society, though.

Public sentiments in Philadelphia as well as in many northern cities firmly opposed not only female participation in the abolitionist movement, but also the ability of women to voice their opinions in mixed gatherings of men and women. Fortunately, Lucretia enjoyed the unconditional support of her husband, James, also a strong women's rights advocate. Although he was less articulate than his wife, James was a pillar of strength for her when she was under attack.[51]

On May 17, 1838, when the Philadelphia Female Anti-Slavery Society held its second meeting, the Motts were nearly killed by a violent white

Lucretia Mott (1793–1880) was Philadelphia's most prominent female reformer. Engraving by John C. Buttre, *c.* 1881. (*Library of Congress*)

mob who railed against the integration of black and white women in that organization. During the proceedings, held at Philadelphia's recently constructed Pennsylvania Hall, the mob set the building on fire. Afterward, the angry hoard began marching towards Mott's house on Sansom Street. Only the quick thinking of several abolitionists, who distracted the mob's attention by shouting "On to the Motts!" and pointing in the wrong directions, prevented further damage.[52]

Such scenes resulted in an inevitable split in the anti-slavery movement between those who refused to mix the issues of slavery and women's rights and those who supported both. When, in 1840, Lucretia found herself barred from the World Anti-Slavery Convention in London, she decided to dedicate herself to the broader principle of equal rights for women as well as for blacks.[53] During the subsequent eight years, Mott and other female Quaker reformers crisscrossed New England, New York, Pennsylvania, and Ohio promoting the dual causes of abolitionism and women's rights.

In July 1848, Mott joined with suffragist Elizabeth Cady Stanton and fellow Quaker Susan B. Anthony to organize a women's rights convention in Seneca Falls, New York.[54] There, Mott drafted a "Declaration of Sentiments" modeled on the Declaration of Independence. The document opened with the premise that "all men and women are created equal" and it indicted men for "endeavoring in every way that he could to destroy [women's] confidence in her own powers, to lessen her self-respect and to make her willing to lead a dependent and abject life."[55]

Seneca Falls was the first in a series of state-wide and national women's rights conventions held across the North in the years preceding the Civil War.[56] The first Pennsylvania State convention was held at West Chester, 25 miles west of Philadelphia, on June 2–3, 1852. Organized by Hannah Darlington, an experienced Quaker abolitionist, the West Chester convention discussed women's suffrage, equal pay, and equal access to education. It also introduced a younger generation of Quaker women— and men—to the cause of women's rights. Among the most prominent members of Philadelphia Yearly Meeting were Mary Ann W. Johnson, Graceanna Lewis, Ann Preston, Jacob Painter, and Evan Pugh.[57]

These conventions would result in the creation of a new organization, the American Equal Rights Association, in 1866, to champion the rights of both women and newly freed slaves, especially the cause of universal suffrage.[58] Lucretia Mott, who served as the organization's president, died in 1880. Although she did not live to see the adoption of the Nineteenth Amendment guaranteeing women the right to vote, she certainly exercised a profound influence on the generation of women who fought to secure that right.[59]

While individual Quakers like Benjamin Lay, Lucretia Mott, Thomas Scattergood, and John Woolman distinguished themselves in the history of social reform, it is important to note that the Society of Friends encourages collective—not individual—leadership. Benevolence has always been foremost a spiritual matter shared by a group of people. New ideas and initiatives evolve from a group search in which all seek to act according to God's will. Even those Friends recognized as "leaders" by the non-Quaker public are viewed, in Quaker circles, as the individuals best able to discern God's message for the group. What matters most to Friends is transforming the idea into action.[60] Not surprisingly, many of the social causes initiated by Philadelphia Quakers have either been adopted by other religious or humanitarian groups or implemented by the federal government for the benefit of all Americans.

Ultimately, Philadelphia's Quaker reformers were content to simply "walk cheerfully over the earth answering that of God in others." This conviction was sorely tested by the American Civil War between 1861 and 1865, forcing Friends to determine how to preserve the Union and effect emancipation without condoning the physical violence and bloodshed of the fratricidal conflict.

A Fiery Trial

On the rainy morning of Sunday, October 26, 1862, President Abraham Lincoln was visited at the Executive Mansion by a small delegation from Philadelphia Yearly Meeting. In the past, Lincoln entertained many similar interviews from religious groups, who came to offer political advice under the guise of divine authority. Occasionally a minister even had the presumptuousness to request an appointment. Although the president felt compelled to endure such meetings, he detested them. On the other hand, he had infinite patience for those who called on a genuinely spiritual mission. Such was the case with the four Quakers who composed the delegation: Eliza P. Gurney, John M. Whitall, Hannah B. Mott, and James Carey. All were deeply affected by the trials of the Civil War and felt a special sympathy for the president in his position of overwhelming responsibility.

Gurney, a Quaker minister, assured Lincoln that it was "not from any motive of idle curiosity" that she and the others requested the interview. Nor did the delegation seek any political favor. Instead, she emphasized the delegation's "near sympathy" for the president in the "heavy weight of responsibility that rested upon him." Quoting from 1 Peter 4:12, the Quaker minister evoked the "fiery trial" experienced by the early Christians who were facing persecution for their faith. She compared Lincoln's circumstances to "God's chosen people," recognizing the "trials and persecutions" he would have to confront because of the war. Gurney urged the president to "commit his way unto the Lord by prayer" whenever those trials emerged. If he did so, she believed that "the peace of God" would "keep the president in heart and mind."

Lincoln was charmed by the innocence and genuine sympathy of Eliza Gurney, who offered a prayer "that light and wisdom might be shed down from on high, to guide our President," before the group settled into a silent meditative worship. When the members of the delegation rose to leave, Lincoln, profoundly affected by the meeting, encouraged the four Friends to stay longer than the fifteen minutes scheduled for their visit. But Gurney declined, noting that the president had too many other responsibilities. Taking her hand, Lincoln, with unusual warmth, confided, "I am glad of this interview."[1]

Afterwards, Lincoln, who was usually guarded about his innermost thoughts, wrote a remarkably candid letter to the Quakeress. After thanking her for her "sympathy and prayer," the president recalled Gurney's sermon and the invocation of Peter's Letter to the early Christians. "We are indeed going through a great trial—a fiery trial," he wrote, wedding his own trial with that of the divided union:

> Your people—the Friends—are also having a very great trial. On principle, and faith, opposed to both war and oppression, they can only practically oppose oppression by war. In this hard dilemma some have chosen one horn and some the other. For those appealing to me on conscientious grounds, I have done, and shall do, the best I could and can, in my own conscience, under my oath to the law. That you believe this, I doubt not; and, believing it, I shall still receive, for our country and myself, your earnest prayers to our Father in Heaven.[2]

Abraham Lincoln (1809–1865) had Quaker ancestors and sympathized with the Friends' desire to free the slaves. Engraving by John C. Buttre, Ridgewood, NJ, 1864. (*Library of Congress*)

The outbreak of the Civil War in 1861 created a trial of principle and faith for Philadelphia Quakers. As pioneers in the anti-slavery movement, Friends hoped to effect emancipation. But as unconditional pacifists they struggled to support a government that was prosecuting a war to achieve the same objective by 1863. President Lincoln, who had Quaker ancestry, sympathized with Friends' dilemma because he faced a similar one, specifically: "How to achieve the desired goal of emancipation without extending the bloodshed as well as emotional and physical hardships of war." Together, Lincoln and the Quakers supported each other in seeking a resolution to their mutual dilemma.[3]

Abraham Lincoln, as president, was influenced by many groups, and it is impossible to determine the precise nature of the Quaker impact on his wartime policies. However, the president was no stranger to the Society of Friends and had great sympathy for as well as a genuine interest in their faith and practice. He was acutely aware of his own Quaker ancestry, noting in his 1860 campaign biography that his "family were originally Quakers, though in later times they have fallen away from the peculiar habits of that people."[4] This knowledge may have inspired him to adopt some of their peculiar practices.

Lincoln exhibited many Quaker traits in his own lifestyle such as refusing to swear oaths, pretending affection, or removing his hat in deference to people in positions of authority. He also demonstrated a preference for simplicity—another quality associated with early Quakers—by dressing in plain black and white clothing, writing speeches, addresses and letters noted for their austerity and brevity, and shunning the use of titles for people, including himself. "Call me Lincoln," he requested, "not Mr. President." Just as appealing to him was the non-doctrinal character of the Quaker faith.[5]

Lincoln did not embrace formal religion. Although he often attended religious services, he rejected his parents' Baptist faith and never claimed membership in a religious denomination. Lincoln tended to rely on reason and personal intellect rather than religious doctrine in his decision-making process. But he was also a man of deep faith who, when faced with a crisis, relied on a sustained personal encounter with God to help him overcome it. That is why Lincoln, during his presidency, became more firmly convinced that behind his own struggles and the Union defeats there was a divine purpose at work.[6] He once confided this belief to Quaker minister Eliza Gurney, writing that he might be an "instrument in the hands of the heavenly Father," and hoped that his "words and actions [as president] may be in accordance with His will."[7] In this sense, Lincoln's spirituality reflected a distinctively Quaker tone, which enabled him to sympathize with Friends and the trial they faced during the Civil War.

Beginning in the 1850s, Philadelphia Quakers realized that their hatred of war and love of freedom were destined to result in a severe trial of principle and faith. Torn between two cherished testimonies, some Friends abandoned their pacifism altogether during the Civil War and voluntarily joined the Union Army. Some of these "Fighting Quakers" were inspired by patriotism and eagerly responded to Lincoln's call for troops. Others were motivated to join the Army of the Potomac by strong abolitionist sentiments and the belief that the means of warfare justified the end of emancipation. Isaac J. Wistar and Norwood Penrose Hallowell, students at Haverford College, enlisted shortly after the Confederate assault on the federal arsenal at Fort Sumter in Charleston Harbor, South Carolina, in April 1861. Wistar, a lieutenant colonel in the California volunteers, served with distinction during the Peninsula campaign and achieved the rank of brigadier general by war's end. Hallowell, a white lieutenant colonel, served as second in command to Colonel Robert Gould Shaw in the 54th Massachusetts, the first African American regiment in the U.S. military.[8] Similarly, some of the older boys at Westtown Friends' Boarding School felt the need to enlist. In November 1861, Joseph Pratt, an eighteen-year-old student, ran away from the school with two classmates to join the Brandywine Guards of the 30th Pennsylvania Regiment.[9]

Although there is no accurate estimate of Friends who enlisted in the Union Army, the radical abolitionist William Lloyd Garrison visiting Philadelphia in 1861 observed that "at least one of nearly every Quaker household was enlisting, much to the concern of Philadelphia Yearly Meeting."[10] Nor is there any accurate estimate of the number of Friends who were disowned for fighting because most of PYM's constituent monthly meetings labored with members who deviated from the peace testimony. They were sensitive to the dilemmas these young Friends faced either between pacifist and abolitionist convictions, or pacifism and the liberty of conscience that had been a cornerstone of Quaker migration to America. Non-Quakers also tended to respect the decision of these young Friends to fight, though they could not fully appreciate the rationale for their decision.[11] "Quakers are drilling, contrary to all the peace principles of the sect," noted one Philadelphian. "May we suppose their hopes to end slavery are based on war!"[12]

On the other hand, the majority of Philadelphia Quakers clung to the peace testimony unconditionally. For the first two years of the Civil War individual Friends as well as committees from Philadelphia's Meetings for Suffering lobbied President Lincoln and his Secretary of War Edwin M. Stanton to exempt those who objected to fighting on religious grounds. Lincoln was more accommodating than Stanton, tending to parole those Quaker resisters who appealed directly to him for an exemption.

In addition, the president often vetoed Stanton's efforts to make Friends accountable to the draft law, forcing his secretary of war to grant exemptions to Quaker resisters on a case-by-case basis. Some were uncompromising pacifists who refused not only to pay money or hire a substitute, but also to perform work that would further the war effort. The latter category included alternative service as a physician, nurse, or orderly because those efforts aimed at putting soldiers back on the battlefront enabling them to take the lives of others. Stanton, widely regarded as an arrogant, stubborn man, showed remarkable patience with these Friends, probably because he was the son of a Quaker physician himself. But he also used his understanding of Quaker faith and practice to refute their arguments, insisting that service in a Union hospital constituted a "work of mercy" and was "in accordance with the commands of Christ."[13]

After Congress passed the first Conscription Act on March 3, 1863, Friends were concerned that the measure did not contain an exemption for conscientious objectors. Many pled their conscience and refused to serve in the Union army, insisting that the Quakers' historic testimony on peace was explicit even against voluntary payment of a fine or for a substitute. When President Lincoln and Secretary of War Edwin Stanton offered to use the $300 commutation fee for a Freedmen's fund or

Secretary of War Edwin Stanton (1814–1869) was strict in enforcing military conscription but was also sympathetic to Quaker conscientious objectors who appealed to him on religious grounds. Engraving by Alexander H. Ritchie, New York, *c.* 1880. (*Library of Congress*)

hospitals, PYM sent a memorial to the president insisting that to pay a fine or to hire a substitute "would be virtually admitting that God is not the sole and sovereign ruler of conscience" and that "human governments may control and coerce [conscience] or withhold the free exercise of it at their pleasure." Lincoln was sympathetic to their plea and pardoned those young Friends who appealed for a religious exemption.[14]

A second draft act, passed at the urging of Lincoln in February 1864, officially exempted religious objectors from military service, providing they did medical work, assisted with recently freed slaves, or paid $300 to be used for the welfare of the freedmen.[15] According to the provision:

> Members of religious denominations, who shall by oath or affirmation declare that they are conscientiously opposed to the bearing of arms, and who are prohibited from doing so by the rules and articles of faith and practice of said religious denominations, shall, when drafted into the military service, be considered non-combatants, and shall be assigned by the Secretary of War to duty in the hospitals, or to the care of freedmen, or shall pay the sum of three hundred dollars ... to be applied to the benefit of the sick and wounded soldiers.[16]

The amendment not only represented the first federal provision of noncombatant service for religious objectors, but a real sacrifice by Lincoln who was struggling to provide the manpower necessary to fight the war.[17] It was a sacrifice that did not go unnoticed by the Quaker minister Eliza Gurney, who had become a valued correspondent of the president.

On September 8, 1864, Gurney wrote to Lincoln thanking him for his "very kind consideration for the religious scruples of the Society of Friends which has been so invariably and generously manifested by the government." Speaking on behalf of her co-religionists, Gurney "ventured to say that Friends are not less loyal for the leniency with which their honest convictions have been treated" and expressed her belief that "there are few among us who would not lament to see any other than Abraham Lincoln fill the presidential chair."[18] But even Gurney could not have appreciated the extent of the sacrifice Lincoln had made by urging Congress to pass such generous terms for conscientious objection.

Just 46,000 men were conscripted into the federal army during the Civil War, and another 118,000 furnished substitutes. Collectively, these 164,000 men along with several thousand from earlier militia drafts made up barely 8 percent of Union troops. Thus, the draft had never been very successful, and by the spring of 1864 volunteering had virtually ceased. War weariness had taken hold in the North. Many soldiers had volunteered for three-year terms, which would expire in 1864. Despite Congressional inducements of bounties and furloughs to those who would re-enlist, at least 100,000 decided not to. The bloody Battle of the Wilderness, fought in early May 1864, resulted in another 17,000 casualties, further discouraging re-enlistment.[19] By allowing Quakers and the members of other peace churches to be exempt from the draft by a commutation fee or alternative service, Lincoln weakened the manpower of the Union army. Viewed in this light, Friends, for better and worse, registered a profound impact on Lincoln's prosecution of the war.

Unfortunately, many recent converts to the Quaker religion sought the same conscientious objector status of birthright Friends but found themselves in the grasp of the Union army being denied an exemption by the federal government. Together with those young Quakers who volunteered for military service, the variety of responses by pacifist Friends indicated a lack of consensus within PYM over its commitment to either the Union war effort or to the discipline of their religious body. These contradictory responses often raised questions within the War Department about the genuineness of the Friends' devotion to pacifism.[20]

Caught in the growing chasm between religious faith and patriotic duty, many Philadelphia Quakers returned to their strength as humanitarian reformers. By alleviating the misery of sick and wounded soldiers and their families and providing for the material relief and education of freedmen, Friends not only achieved a resolution to their own spiritual trial, but redemption in the larger society which had criticized them for refusing to fight.

Initially, Philadelphia Quakers responded by contributing to the comfort of sick and wounded soldiers as well as to the welfare of Union widows and orphans. Some distributed food, bandages, sheets, or warm clothing which they had collected or made themselves. Others ministered to the spiritual needs of Union soldiers and among Confederate prisoners of war. Lucretia Mott preached at Camp William Penn, a training center for U.S. Colored Troops, though she stressed her belief that the time would come when war would be no more. Mott's granddaughter, Maria Hopper, along with her aunt, Abby Hopper Gibbons, volunteered as nurses at Union army hospitals.[21] Such humanitarian work earned pacifist Friends the respect and admiration of the military as reflected by the statement of one army chaplain who, after observing Quaker efforts, noted: "I saw the difference between talking Christianity and acting it."[22]

Philadelphia Quakers also provided material relief of recently freed slaves. Working with Freedmen's Aid associations, Friends, both Hicksite and Orthodox, were among the most active groups in freedmen's relief. The city's Hicksite Friends formed a Women's Aid Society in April 1862, which later worked with the National Freedmen's Relief Association, raising

Camp William Penn, training camp for black troops enlisted into the United States Army, located in Cheltenham Township, Montgomery County, Pa. Unknown artist. Taken from Frank H. Taylor, *Philadelphia in the Civil War, 1861–1865* (1913), p. 184.

$349,000 for work in camps near Vicksburg, Mississippi, and at Helena, Arkansas. A year later, the Friends Freedmen's Association was organized by some of the most prominent Orthodox families of the city, including the Copes, Cadburys, Shipleys, and Scattergoods. Not to be outdone, Hicksite Quakers, in 1864, established the Friends Association for the Aid and Elevation of the Freedmen. Both organizations raised money for food and shelter, collected clothing, and sent generous contributions to give former slaves a start in free society.[23] Even Lucretia Mott, famous for understatement, could not contain her enthusiasm for these efforts. "We are really beginning to do something," she gushed, "the Biddles, the Parrishes, Whartons, and such like [are] alive to the subject!"[24]

Although Orthodox and Hicksite Friends tended to work separately, they did occasionally cooperate in aid to the Freedmen. In 1865, when newly freed slaves began to arrive in Philadelphia in record numbers, the two groups worked with the Pennsylvania Abolition Society in funding an office to find jobs and homes for the refugees.[25]

Other Philadelphia Quakers traveled South to establish schools for the religious and educational instruction of the freedmen and their children. They assisted federal efforts by establishing the Port Royal Relief Committee in 1862. The committee set about finding teachers for these former slaves, many of whom were Quakers. The very first school for freedmen—the Penn School on St. Helena Island, South Carolina— was also established in 1862 and sponsored by Philadelphia Friends. The Penn School, named after William Penn, was an important outgrowth of the federal government's "Port Royal Experiment" on South Carolina's Sea Islands. Designed to demonstrate that the freedmen were capable of self-sufficiency, the experiment paired government funding with private philanthropy to ensure its initial success. Although the Penn School was not a Quaker institution per se, money and supplies came at various times from the Friends Freedmen's Association and individual Quakers, and most of the trustees were Friends. Within three years, the school was sending teachers of African descent into the surrounding area to open schools of their own. In 1864 alone, the Friends Freedmen's Association of Philadelphia provided for the education of 3,700 pupils and another 21,200 Sunday school students in Virginia.[26]

Lincoln, impressed by the Friends' work with newly freed slaves, urged Congress in the spring of 1865 to establish the government's own "Freedmen's Bureau" to further such efforts. Approved by Congress in March 1865, the federal agency provided material aid, education, and relocation for the thousands of refugees living in the South. It also provided financial and material assistance to Quaker relief organizations in establishing schools for freedmen.[27]

Philadelphia Quakers' work for the relief of the freedmen represented a watershed in the history of American Quakerism. Compassion for the suffering of African slaves and a fierce commitment to social justice had thrust Friends into the forefront of the abolition movement in the late seventeenth century where they remained for nearly two centuries. At times, their efforts were praised. On other occasions, when their Underground Railroad activities violated federal law, Friends were

Believing that education was a key to the future of newly freed slaves, Philadelphia Quakers founded schools in the South to teach Freedmen and their children the rudiments of literacy. Engraving by L. Stebbins, Hartford, CT, 1866. Taken from John T. Trowbridge, *The South: A Tour of its Battlefields and Ruined Cities* (1866), p. 339. (*Library of Congress*)

denounced by the general public and, when caught, prosecuted by state and federal authorities. Humanitarian aid to freedmen, however, allowed Friends to express their loyalty to the Union in a practical way and one in which they had traditionally excelled. Instead of challenging the government, Quakers were cooperating with it to further the cause of human freedom. Their relief work for Freedmen had allowed Friends to redeem themselves for whatever criticism they had suffered in placing their peace principles above patriotism.[28]

Despite their considerable humanitarian efforts, Friends could not guarantee that their president would win re-election in 1864. Mounting casualty rates, division within the Republican Party over the president's emancipation policy, and public doubts about his leadership jeopardized his chances for a second term. Predictably, Lincoln was not the unanimous choice of the Republicans for the nomination since a mix of radicals, abolitionists and disappointed office-seekers favored General John C. Fremont. These disgruntled factions hoped to divide the Republican Party with a platform calling for a constitutional amendment ending slavery. Only after several prominent Republican businessmen and professionals, including Quaker newspaper editor John G. Whittier, convinced Fremont to "stand aside for the greater number in the party," did he agree to end his candidacy.[29] Even then, Lincoln's re-election was far from certain, though he did secure the dissenters' desired constitutional amendment in his party's platform. The president was running against his former commanding general, the highly popular George B. McClellan, who was nominated by the Democrats. Nor was the war going well, with Union forces unable to make any significant gains during the spring and summer of 1864.[30]

Although Lincoln's bid for re-election was threatened by his detractors, he also enjoyed a solid base of supporters, including many Friends. In addition to Whittier, who discouraged Fremont's candidacy, Lincoln enjoyed the on-going support of Quaker minister Eliza Gurney, who, by September 1864, was addressing her letters to him "Esteemed Friend." Gurney spoke to the president's spiritual needs during this time, assuring him that "in thy time of trouble a gracious God who comforts all that mourn will continue to sustain and strengthen, uphold and comfort thee." Urging Lincoln to find solace in his Christian faith, the Quaker minister reminded him that the "believer in Jesus will have a holy calm, peace with God, a deep, still undercurrent of soul-satisfying happiness which even the rudest storms of time cannot fail to disturb." She repeated her firm belief that the president was chosen by God "to fulfill the important trust of achieving an unbroken Union where the oppressed are set free." Gurney concluded the letter by assuring the president that most Quakers felt that he was "conscientiously endeavoring to fulfill the solemn duties of his high

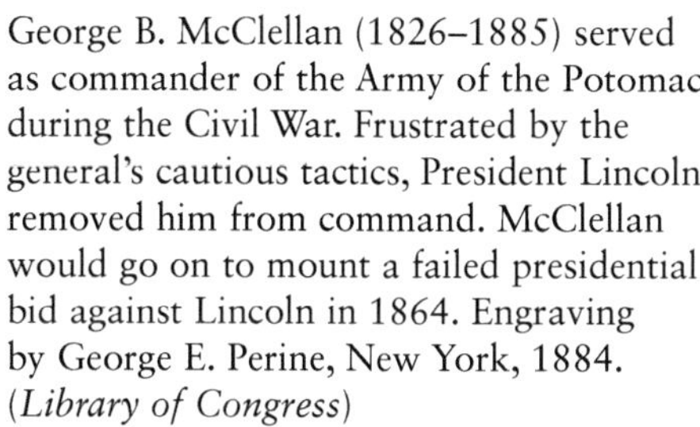

George B. McClellan (1826–1885) served as commander of the Army of the Potomac during the Civil War. Frustrated by the general's cautious tactics, President Lincoln removed him from command. McClellan would go on to mount a failed presidential bid against Lincoln in 1864. Engraving by George E. Perine, New York, 1884. (*Library of Congress*)

and responsible office according to his own convictions of right" and that he would enjoy their support in the "next Presidential election."[31]

Similarly, Lincoln, meeting with the female officers of the Philadelphia Sanitary Commission to thank them for their service, was consoled by a Quaker member. She could see the heavy toll the war had taken on him and, taking his hand in hers, she said: "Friend Abraham, thee need not think thee stands alone. We are all praying for thee. All our hearts, the hearts of all people, are behind thee and thee cannot fail. The Lord has appointed thee and He will sustain thee. Take comfort, friend Abraham, God is with thee."

Noticeably moved by her words, Lincoln admitted that it had been a "bad day," and that he had "almost forgotten that the hearts of all loyal people are with me." "If I didn't have that knowledge," he added, "and the knowledge that God is sustaining and will sustain me until my appointed work is done, I could not endure it. My heart would have broken long ago." Thanking the Quakeress for her kindness, he turned to the other women and said, "God bless you all."[32]

Lincoln's fortunes changed as the presidential campaign unfolded. McClellan, who supported a continuation of the war and restoration of the Union, was forced to repudiate the Democratic Party's platform, which called for an immediate cessation of hostilities and a negotiated settlement with the Confederacy. The act divided the Democrats and made McClellan's success at the polls remote at best. Union military success in the autumn of 1864, highlighted by the fall of Atlanta, also boosted Northern support for Lincoln's prosecution of the war. Thus, the president won re-election easily with 212 electoral votes to McClellan's twenty-one and a popular vote margin of 403,000, or 55 percent.[33] Armed with such a popular mandate, Lincoln was determined to complete the work of emancipation.

Although he had freed the slaves by executive order with the Emancipation Proclamation on January 1, 1863, it was done as a "wartime necessity" implemented by his broadly defined powers as commander-in-chief. Thus, the Proclamation was a temporary measure that could easily be overturned by the courts after the war ended. If the Civil War ended without a constitutional amendment ending slavery, the very purpose of the war would be undermined and the Union soldiers who sacrificed their lives would die in vain. The Senate had already passed such an amendment the previous spring, but there were not enough Republicans in the House to provide the two-thirds majority required for passage in that branch of Congress. The main obstacle was the pro-slavery Democrats, who would eagerly embrace a peace settlement realizing that it would undermine the campaign for emancipation. But Lincoln prevailed by securing the necessary votes from the opposition party before the war ended.[34]

On January 31, 1865, the U.S. House of Representatives narrowly reached the two-thirds majority needed to pass the bill by a vote of 119 to fifty-six. Afterwards, the amendment was sent to the state legislatures where the Northern states quickly ratified it. Although the formal adoption of the amendment would not come until December 6, 1865, Lincoln had redeemed himself in the eyes of African Americans, endeared himself to the Quakers for all time, and secured his place in history as the "Great Emancipator."[35]

While it is impossible to determine the exact degree of influence Philadelphia Quakers may have had on President Lincoln's decision-making and wartime policies, their relationship was based on a mutual trust inspired by a mutual respect and the understanding that human beings are instruments of the Divine will. Together, Lincoln and the Quakers supported each other throughout the Civil War in seeking a resolution to a similar trial of principle and faith, specifically how to achieve emancipation while ending the bloody carnage of war.

Philadelphia Friends met with the president and wrote to him constantly, offering their prayers, urging emancipation, and assisting with the education and relief of freed slaves. In fact, Lincoln's association and cooperation with Quakers became so common during the war that many Friends felt as if they enjoyed a special relationship with the president, so special that they addressed him as "friend."

When he was assassinated on April 14, 1865, Quakers felt as if they had lost one of their own. Not before or since Lincoln's administration has the Religious Society of Friends been as devoted to a United States president.

6

Winds of Change

The period between the Civil War and the turn of the nineteenth century witnessed the transformation of Philadelphia into an industrial giant due to the natural abundance and accessibility of coal and iron in other parts of Pennsylvania. Leading industries like the Pennsylvania Railroad, Baldwin Locomotive, Cramp & Sons Ship and Engine Building Company, and Lukens Steel dominated the city's economy, prospering alongside an array of textile mills and factories whose diversity was scarcely matched anywhere else in the nation. The Quaker city was also home to small and mid-sized firms. Textile businesses, for example, ranged from a cottage industry to larger factories with flexible strategies for production and networks of linked specializations with spinning, weaving, dyeing, and finishing often performed in separate establishments.[1]

The Centennial Exposition of 1876 held in Fairmount Park introduced the world to new industrial and technological advancements such as the telephone, automatic telegraph system, mechanical calculator, and Corliss steam engine.[2] No longer a center of politics or religion, Philadelphia assumed a new role as a leader in technology and business.

A new city hall, begun in 1871, reflected the emerging status as well as the exuberance and excess of the Gilded Age. With its highly ornate decoration, the edifice reflected the Second Empire style popular in France, looking more like a Baroque castle than a government building. At the same time, the structure's enormous granite walls fronted by 88 million bricks, and thousands of tons of white marble and limestone represented the most recent technology in urban architecture and the embodiment of the industrial era.

When completed in 1901, City Hall was 548 feet above street level and contained 700 rooms dedicated for uses of various governmental operations making it the largest municipal building in the United States. It was also the tallest habitable building in the world until 1908 when New York City's Singer Office Building surpassed it.[3]

Philadelphia's City Hall, begun in 1872, was the world's tallest habitable building at 548 feet when completed in 1901 and reflected the Industrial era in which it was constructed. Engraving taken from North American Publishing and Engraving Company, *Illustrated Philadelphia Its Wealth and Industries* (1889), p. 35. (*Public Domain*)

Despite the opulence of the new City Hall—or perhaps because of it—the Quaker businessmen and civic leaders who sat on the Commission of Public Buildings hoped to honor William Penn's legacy by including him in the construction. In one of their most ambitious, if not shameless, efforts, the commissioners, in June 1881, attempted to bring Penn's body back to Philadelphia from its quiet resting place at Jordan's Burial Ground in Buckinghamshire, England, and have it reinterred inside the courtyard of the new castle-like structure. The commissioners concocted the scheme along with Pennsylvania Governor Henry M. Hoyt to highlight the bicentennial celebration of Pennsylvania's founding scheduled for 1882.[4]

Hoyt appointed building commissioner George L. Harrison to negotiate the transfer. When Harrison met with Penn's heirs and the British government, he justified the measure by reasoning that Penn's work was "almost forgotten in his native country of England," but that the "5 million people who profit by his sacrifices are ready to offer him that tribute of whole-hearted reverence by transferring his remains to Philadelphia."[5] After securing their approval, Harrison met with the Quaker trustees of Jordan's Meeting House and Burial Ground, who retained legal custody of Penn's remains.[6] This time, he was not successful.

The trustees denied his request insisting that Jordan's was "selected by William Penn as the burial place of himself and his family during the vigor of life." They also stated their concern that the transfer of Penn's remains would be accompanied by "a State ceremonial, military honors and a

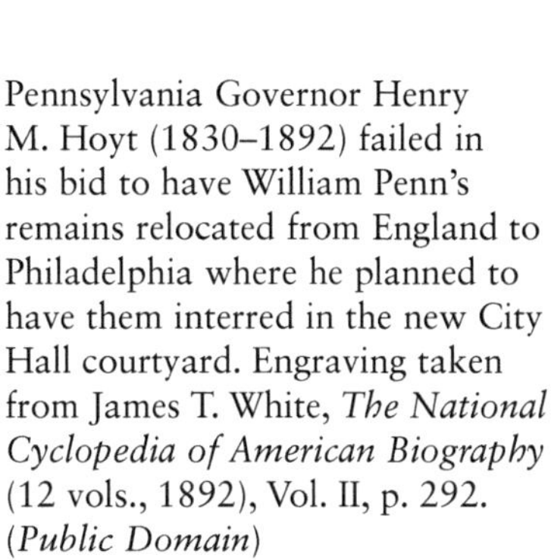

Pennsylvania Governor Henry M. Hoyt (1830–1892) failed in his bid to have William Penn's remains relocated from England to Philadelphia where he planned to have them interred in the new City Hall courtyard. Engraving taken from James T. White, *The National Cyclopedia of American Biography* (12 vols., 1892), Vol. II, p. 292. (*Public Domain*)

parade" and the new location would bear an "elaborate, monumental tombstone." Such "pomp and circumstance," they argued, "would be utterly repugnant to Penn's known character and sentiments, which favored Quaker simplicity."[7]

Having failed in their efforts, the commissioners went ahead with their plan for a bronze statue of William Penn to be placed atop the new City Hall. Alexander Milne Calder, the European sculptor hired to complete most of the figurative architecture for the building in 1873, was retained to do the statue. But his workload would not allow him to concentrate on the project until 1886. Even then, the statue took him nearly six years to finish. Cast at the Tacony Iron Works in Northeast Philadelphia, the 37-foot, 53,348-pound figure was completed in 1892 and depicts a youthful and dignified proprietor dressed in fashionable seventeenth-century attire. In his left hand, Penn holds the Charter of Privileges, and with the other, he extends a blessing of peace and friendship over his beloved city.[8]

On November 28, 1894, after standing on display in the courtyard for two years, the statue was hoisted to the top of the clock tower in fourteen sections. It was placed facing northeast, looking toward Penn Treaty Park, where the Quaker proprietor allegedly made a treaty with the Lenni Lenape Indians more than two centuries earlier. While Penn himself would have probably liked the placement of his statue, he certainly would not appreciate the fact that it provided the finishing touch for a monument to the graft-ridden Republican machine that built City Hall. Nor would Penn's practical taste in architecture tolerate the craggy magnificence of the structure, which one architect claimed, "combines bulk with sterling insignificance, squalid paltriness and painfully grotesque decorations."[9] Nevertheless, City Hall continues to serve as a reminder of Philadelphia's industrial era.

Just as enduring was the Friends' reputation for benevolence and financial success. While their many philanthropic activities gave the city's Quakers a well-deserved reputation for "doing good," their business acumen allowed them to also "do well" financially. According to merchant Joshua Baily, the key to the Friends' business success was "keeping their capital in their own businesses and not doing more business than their capital warranted."[10] Although such a conservative investment policy prevented rapid growth, it did offer Quaker-owned businesses healthy long-range stability. Consider the example of the Provident Life and Trust Company founded by Orthodox Friends in 1865.

Controlled by an exclusively Quaker board, the Provident, which insured lives, granted annuities, and administered trusts, began modestly in rented quarters with second-hand furniture. The company required careful medical examinations to determine whether to insure those who applied for insurance. They also selected agents for their integrity rather than aggressive salesmanship. Within six years, the company purchased its own building on South Fourth Street and boasted an insurance income of $503,902 and insurance in force totaling $9 million. Two years later, during the Panic of 1873 when other insurance firms were forced to close their doors, the Provident continued its steady growth. By 1878, the company's total insurance in force had risen to $21 million.

In the 1880s, when other insurance companies adopted the "deferred dividend" plan to increase volume exponentially, the Provident retained its annual dividends policy believing that too rapid economic growth would undermine security. They proved to be correct in 1905 when deferred dividends were outlawed. Operating with caution, the Provident continued its steady and substantial growth, which amounted to $316 million insurance in force by 1915.[11]

Strawbridge & Clothier's, a Quaker-operated retail dry goods business, is another fine example of the Friends' business ethic. The venture began in 1868 as a partnership between Justus Clayton Strawbridge, an Orthodox Friend, and Isaac Hallowell Clothier, a Hicksite. Operating at Eighth and Market Streets with a budget of $54,000, the partners did business on a cash-only basis. In that way, they did not suffer any financial loss from customers who purchased with credit and later reneged on payment. The strategy also benefited paying customers who otherwise would have been charged an additional tax by the store to help pay off the debt accrued from the delinquents.

Strawbridge & Clothier's also kept their percentage of profit low in the interest of a rapid turnover of the ever-increasing variety of domestic and imported dry goods they carried. They also insisted on a fixed price for all the items they sold to avoid bargaining with customers. While these policies resulted in immediate success, allowing the store to expand west on Market Street, they also forced the two partners to abandon their strict policy against credit purchases. As a result, the store began to sell a wider variety of products other than dry goods and expanded to a chain of stores so rapidly that its annual income rose to $10 million by 1900.[12]

There were other Quaker businessmen who fit the stereotype of "robber baron," or industrialists and financiers who made fortunes by monopolizing huge industries. Since there were no federal regulations prohibiting such practices at the time, these entrepreneurs created trusts that combined several industries to secure their personal fortunes. Clement Acton Griscom, a Hicksite Quaker, was one of these. Born in 1841 to a long-established Quaker family, Griscom, at age sixteen, went to work as a clerk at Peter Wright and Sons, a Quaker shipping firm in Philadelphia. He became a partner in the business in 1863 after winning transport contracts from the oil industry, which transformed the company into a major shipping firm.

Griscom's dealings introduced him to prominent financiers Marcus Hanna and John D. Rockefeller, who provided the funding and counsel to establish the International Navigation Company. By 1888, the company

Clement A. Griscom (1841–1912) was a Quaker Robber Barron and the key figure in American transatlantic shipping by 1900. Engraving taken from Mitchell C. Harrison, *Prominent and Progressive Americans* (2 vols., 1902), Vol. I, p. 142.

had absorbed two other shipping lines—the Red Star Line of Belgium and the American Line, which handled all shipping between the East Coast and the British ports of Liverpool and Southampton. During the next decade, Griscom's ships plied the Atlantic Ocean between Philadelphia, Antwerp, and England making him a multi-millionaire and the key figure in American transatlantic shipping.[13]

Joseph Wharton was another Quaker industrialist who made a fortune on mines, steel, and railroads. In 1853, Wharton, at age twenty-seven, joined the Pennsylvania and Lehigh Railroad as a manager of their subsidiary mining operation. Three years later, he began to buy into Bethlehem Iron Company which produced pig iron and steel rails. Over the next twenty years, Wharton gradually invested more of his own time and energy in the company. He would eventually purchase a controlling share of the company.

In 1885, Wharton successfully bid a contract with the United States Navy for forged steel armor. The next year, he visited England and France to research the designs for a plant to forge steel of higher quality. With these designs, Bethlehem Iron built the first plant to forge high-strength steel in America. The plant fabricated armor plates and guns for warships and soon became the largest producer of pig iron in the country. Together with his extensive iron and coal mines and refining works, Bethlehem Iron, later renamed "Bethlehem Steel," made Wharton one of the wealthiest men on the East Coast.[14]

It is more difficult to ascertain the attitude Philadelphia's wealthy Quaker businessmen had towards the urban poor. On one hand, they, like their seventeenth-century ancestors, appeared to treat the poor with the same compassion and disinterested benevolence. Whether Hicksite or Orthodox, the Quaker aristocracy agreed on the responsibilities of their wealth. During the 1890s when the nation was in the throes of a disastrous depression, these affluent Friends met their obligation to the less advantaged by channeling their philanthropy into the same benevolent activities of their ancestors including prison reform, care of the mentally ill and the poor and education. One wealthy Friend, Anna T. Jeanes, was among the most prominent Quaker benefactors of the time.

The youngest of ten children born to Isaiah and Anna Thomas Jeanes, Anna's father and two brothers, Samuel and Joshua, were wealthy Philadelphia merchants. A third brother, Joseph, was a coal magnate. Her only sister, Mary, was a philanthropist and abolitionist. Since Anna never married and her siblings died childless, she inherited the family's fortune. She also understood that with great privilege came great responsibility and was determined to give away her inheritance to charity.[15]

Deeply affected by the human suffering caused by the Civil War, reconstruction, and the massive migration of European immigrants and blacks to the industrial north, Jeanes carefully and wisely donated her finances to institutions that lessened human suffering in a rapidly changing industrial society. Education was one of her favorite charities.[16] She gave $500,000 to the Spring Garden Institute, a technical school in Philadelphia, and another $200,000 to the city's Friends schools. In addition, Jeanes' bequest of $1,000,000 funded the Negro Rural School Fund, which appointed Booker T. Washington as a trustee.[17] The fund supported the training of black teachers who provided southern black youth with academic and vocational education.

Concerned by the burdens of life experienced by immigrants, the poor, and the displaced, Anna donated more than $1,000,000 to the following organizations: the Penn Asylum for Widows and Single Women; Homes for Destitute Colored Children; Homes for the Aged and Infirm Colored Persons; Firemen's Pension Fund; Pennsylvania Working and Industrial Homes for Blind Men; Pennsylvania Society to Prevent Cruelty to Children; Sanitarium Association of Philadelphia (for sick children); soup kitchens; and children's nurseries.[18]

Unwilling to live alone on her family's large estate, Anna, at age seventy-two, built a boarding home "for aged Quakers and those in sympathy with us." Not satisfied with one, she personally supervised and carefully monitored the finances and building of a second named "Stapeley" in the Germantown neighborhood of Philadelphia into which she moved. When she was diagnosed with breast cancer in the last year of her life, Anna left her entire residuary estate to Philadelphia Yearly Meeting to build "a general hospital for cancerous, nervous and disabling ailments." Opened in 1929, Jeanes Hospital is located on the former Jeanes family farm in the Fox Chase section of Northeast Philadelphia. Consistent with Anna's will, the Institute for Cancer Research and American Oncologic Hospital later relocated to the Jeanes campus. These two institutions eventually merged to become Fox Chase Cancer Center.[19]

While Anna Jeanes's efforts were motivated by disinterested benevolence, some historians believe that other members of Philadelphia's Quaker aristocracy were more concerned about social control. The unbridled growth of Philadelphia's manufacturing economy was accompanied by a significant increase in crime, poverty and truancy that needed to be addressed. If not, those urban ills would threaten the prosperity of the city's Quaker businessmen. The public schools, for example, would keep idle immigrant children off the streets and provide the rudiments of literacy to prepare them for employment in the city's factories. Similarly, workhouses, homes for the destitute and temperance organizations would serve to break the vicious cycle between crime and poverty. These were the same reasons that compelled the city's wealthiest Friends to relocate to the suburbs at the turn of the century.[20]

Hoping to escape the social ills that plagued industrial Philadelphia, the Quaker elite relocated to communities along the Pennsylvania Railroad's Main Line to Paoli and its commuter route to Media. Haverford, Lansdowne, Merion, and Swarthmore were the preferred destinations. Thus, the Quaker aristocracy was able to commute daily into the city to run their businesses and then return home to the countryside in the evening.[21]

However, evidence of the Quaker motive for controlling the behavior of the urban poor is circumstantial. Generally, the poor and working-class immigrants who flooded Philadelphia during the late nineteenth and early twentieth centuries depended upon their own institutions, especially churches, for support as well as for assimilating into American society. Along with family and job, religion was the focal point of immigrant life. For Poles, Czechs, and the Irish, the Catholic Church not only provided spiritual support, but education as well as social services for their immigrant parishioners. For German and Russian Jews, the synagogue did the same. Priests and rabbis found employment for their congregants, interceded on their behalf in legal disputes when necessary, and introduced them to the complexities of urban industrial America.[22] Thus, Philadelphia's immigrant community did not require the charity of wealthy Quakers.

On the other hand, there is no question that social control was a major objective of Philadelphia Friends' work with Native Americans at the turn of the century. The belief in the nobility of the Indian that had inspired the seventeenth-century Quaker efforts to befriend the Delaware tribes had yielded to a firm conviction in the necessity of assimilation by 1870. Pressured by Friends to reject a military solution, President Ulysses S. Grant decided to experiment with relocating the western tribes on reservations. Impressed by the Friends' concern for Native Americans and hoping to put an end to the mistreatment of the tribes, Grant appointed the Indian committees of the two Philadelphia Yearly Meetings to supervise some 25,000 reservation Indians in Nebraska and Kansas.[23]

Members of the Hicksite Yearly Meeting's Indian Committee staffed and directed two Nebraska agencies. Thomas Lightfoot went to the Great Nehama Agency where the Iowa and Sac and Fox tribes were living, and Albert L. Green was assigned to the Otoe Agency. Between 1869 and 1879, Lightfoot and Green secured $60,000 as well as clothing and supplies for their respective agencies from Philadelphia's Hicksite Quakers.[24] Orthodox Friends had a more limited involvement on reservations in Kansas. Nor were they as successful as the Hicksites, raising approximately $30,000 in the same ten-year span.[25]

In addition to collecting supplies and raising money, the Hicksite and Orthodox Indian agencies were responsible for educating the tribes in white ways of speaking, dressing, personal hygiene, and grooming. That meant discouraging tribal practices such as a nomadic lifestyle, sharing common property, speaking their native language, and dressing in native clothing. Seeking to transform their Indian charges into small, landholding farmers, Lightfoot and Green tried to teach the Indians English, to dress in western clothing, to work hard, save their earnings, and respect private property. It was a mixed success at best.[26]

Many of the adult males refused to abandon their Indian culture and became unruly. When this occurred, Lightfoot and Green had no choice but to turn them over to the military to enforce their directives through corporal punishment. Not only did this practice violate the Quaker belief in pacifism, but it weakened authority on the agencies by dividing it between Friends and the military.[27]

In 1877, President Rutherford Hayes buckled under political pressure from western settlers and the U.S. Army, who demanded a tougher Indian policy, and abandoned Grant's reservation experiment. By 1885, Hicksite and Orthodox involvement on the Nebraska and Kansas agencies had ended.[28]

Philadelphia Quakers were more reluctant to address the corrupt Republican machine that dominated city politics. United States Senator Matthew S. Quay controlled the state and city political machinery by dispensing contracts, patronage, and campaign funds. His genius for election fixing and voter fraud was unparalleled among all other big-city bosses of the Gilded Age. Quay allied his Republican machine with Philadelphia's saloons, gambling dens, and other commercial vice operations, which helped bring out the vote and paid protection money that helped fund the party's bribes and services. Even the Democratic Party was on the take. Quay's machine paid the rent on the Democrats' headquarters and guaranteed them a percentage of offices to make it appear as if a genuine two-party system functioned. To ensure the fix, city police beat citizens or elections officers who tried to do their duty and then charged them with inciting a riot.[29]

"Deprived of self-government, Philadelphians take their orders from the state boss, Matthew S. Quay, who is the proprietor of Pennsylvania and the real ruler of Philadelphia, just as William Penn, the Great Proprietor, was," wrote muckraking journalist Lincoln Steffens in the July 1903 issue of *McClure's Magazine*. "Other American cities, no matter how bad their own condition may be, all point with scorn to Philadelphia as the worst-governed city in the country. But I believe that Philadelphia is simply the most corrupt and the most contented to remain that way."[30]

Wealthy Friends shied away from confronting Quay because of their longtime attachment to the Republican Party as well as the Friends'

Matthew S. Quay (1833–1904) was a United States senator and party boss of Philadelphia's corrupt Republican machine in the 1880s. Engraving taken from John W. Hanson, *The History of Our Great Parties, Men and Political Issues* (1896), p. 372. (*Public Domain*)

tradition of avoiding active participation in politics. But in the 1870s, middle-class Quaker liberals began to take a stand against the corrupt Republican machine and encourage other Friends to become involved in city politics.

Thomas Speakman, a Hicksite Friend, condemned Quay for "ostracizing and excluding the best qualified and most worthy men from public places." He urged Hicksites "to restore governmental affairs to something like their original purity."[31] Orthodox Friend Rufus Jones also urged his brethren to abandon their political hesitancy and take an active part in politics. He backed his words by serving for many years as a Republican committeeman.[32] Heeding their advice, Clement Biddle and T. Wistar Brown were among the several Quakers who founded the "Committee of 100" that initiated civil service reform. Exposing the corrupt practices of the Quay machine, the committee succeeded in bouncing dishonest Republicans from municipal office and electing reform-minded Democrat officials, including Samuel G. King who was elected mayor in 1881.[33]

Unfortunately, Quaker efforts at political reform ended with King's victory. The Republican machine was too strong and too influential to be defeated. After Quay's death in 1904, his successor, U.S. Senator Boies Penrose, assumed leadership of the corrupt machine. A descendant of the Quaker merchant aristocracy, Penrose's shameless appetite for political

Boies Penrose (1860–1921), who was born into a prominent Philadelphia Quaker family, succeeded Matthew Quay as the party boss of the city's corrupt Republican machine. Engraving by Edward G. Williams, New York, 1889. (*Library of Congress*)

power spurred him to serve the industrial tycoons of the era through backroom deals, election fixing, and the spoils system until his death in 1921.[34]

The secularizing influences and pressures of the marketplace were not limited to Philadelphia's Quaker aristocracy, either. While these captains of industry played an instrumental role in the economy of the nation's second largest city, Friends who belonged to the more substantial middle class were not immune to the worldliness of the Gilded Age. It was extremely difficult for them to maintain, or defend, such Quaker principles as simplicity and equality when those virtues were out of step with the times. Some left the Quaker religion for other religious denominations. Others allowed their membership to lapse. Still others attempted to reconcile their Quaker principles with secular society. These trends not only resulted in declining membership within Philadelphia Yearly Meeting but also a noticeable decline of Quaker distinctiveness in Friends schools and colleges.

Many of the Friends schools that had been established in the eighteenth and early nineteenth centuries to provide a guarded education for Quaker youth had disappeared by the 1870s due to a lack of students and financial support. In 1875, the Orthodox Quaker Overseers of the Friends Public School consolidated their remaining neighborhood schools into a single college-preparatory day school for boys named "William Penn Charter." Located at 8 South 12th St., the new school gained a national reputation for high quality instruction. To prevent their male students from leaving for the public schools, which had established competitive sports programs, Penn Charter, in 1887, introduced interscholastic football, track, and baseball, and co-founded with Germantown Academy the Inter-Academic Athletic Association for private schools.[35]

The abandonment of a Quaker educational tradition was especially troubling to Hicksite Friends who viewed urban life as an evil. To address the concern, the Hicksites, in 1893, established a boarding school in rural Bucks County. Known as the "George School," the institution emphasized a guarded education, and the student body was limited to those who had at least one parent who was a member of a Hicksite meeting.[36] Westtown, founded in 1799 as a boarding school and operated by Orthodox Friends, also renewed its commitment to a guarded education by accepting as students only those children who could claim both parents as members of Orthodox meetings. At both boarding schools, the curriculum emphasized practical subjects, such as mathematics, science, grammar, and writing. The reading program focused on Scripture, non-fiction, and English literature. Fiction, poetry, and drama were prohibited. Also absent were school theatrical plays and music.[37] But the two boarding schools were exceptions in their efforts to retain a guarded education.

With the growing secularization of Quaker education, the city's remaining Friends schools and were forced to adopt a different mission. Instead of providing a guarded education strictly for the children of Friends, the schools opened their doors to non-Quakers with the mission of exposing greater numbers of Philadelphians to Friends' principles. In 1890, for example, three-fifths of the students enrolled at the recently consolidated Friends Select School founded by the Orthodox came from other Protestant denominations. At Friends Central, founded by the Hicksites, the non-Quaker enrollment was even higher consisting of four-fifths of the total student body.[38] As the numbers of non-Quaker students rose, the pressure to abandon Friends' traditions and practices also increased. The trend also affected the three Quaker colleges.

Prior to the 1830s, there was little Quaker interest in higher education. While other religious denominations founded colleges in the early nineteenth century, the Society of Friends saw no need for such institutions because of the emphasis on educating clergy, which ran counter to the Quaker belief in a lay ministry. In the mid-nineteenth century, however, higher education was becoming more secularized, preparing students for professions in law, medicine, and teaching. At least a few Philadelphia Quakers had enrolled in non-Quaker colleges like Harvard, Amherst,

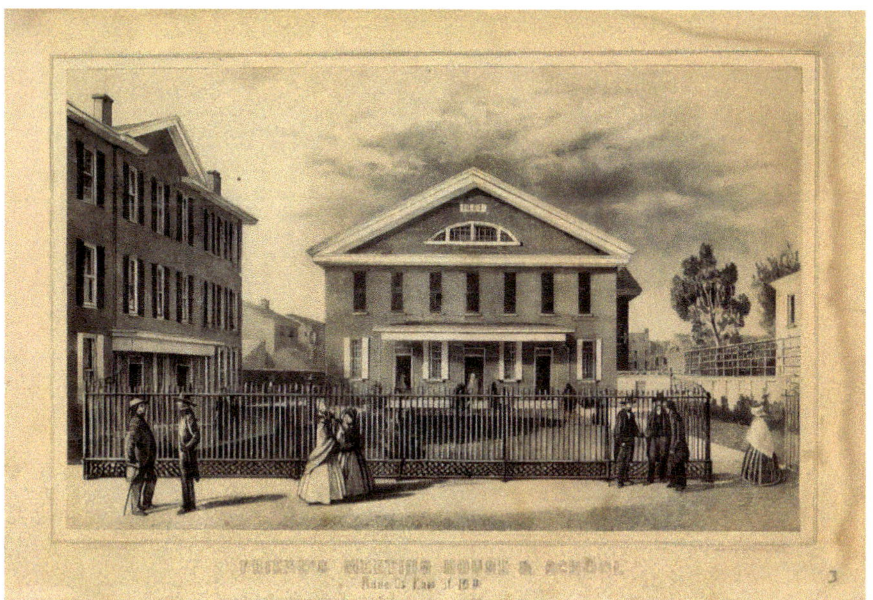

By 1890, Friends Central School, like most of Philadelphia's Quakers schools, was serving a majority of non-Quaker students. Unknown artist. (*Library Company of Philadelphia*)

and Bowdoin to train for these professions. Initially, Philadelphia Yearly Meeting abandoned its hostility to higher education to prepare young Quakers to teach in the Friends schools. In 1833, Haverford College was established outside the city limits for this purpose. Other Quaker colleges followed at Swarthmore (1864) and Bryn Mawr (1885).[39]

If the intent of these colleges was to preserve the Quaker tradition, the founders were sorely disappointed. The three colleges proved to be much less resistant to the wider culture than the elementary and secondary schools. In fact, they became agents of change within the Society of Friends. Not only were the colleges open to non-Quakers, but they encouraged professions other than teaching, including those in business, literature, and the fine arts. In the 1880s, Haverford College built such a strong liberal arts curriculum that it ceased teaching courses in education altogether. Students were required to take Greek and Latin in each of their four years on campus. Outside pressures also forced the college to offer engineering. In addition, Haverford as well as Bryn Mawr and Swarthmore improved the quality of instruction by attracting prominent non-Quaker scholars to their faculties. By the beginning of the twentieth century, the three Friends colleges had become elite national institutions as the proportion of Quaker students and faculty declined.[40]

Haverford College, founded in 1833, had become an elite small college for young men, most of whom were non-Quaker. Unknown artist. (*Lower Merion Historical Society, Bala Cynwyd, PA*)

At the turn of the nineteenth century, Philadelphia Quakers were forced to confront the issue of proper Christian responsibility in a burgeoning industrial society. While they tried to preserve their identity as a peculiar people and remain aloof from the secularizing influences of the mainstream, Friends yielded to the winds of change, which favored big business and civil service reform. Never completely at ease with such worldly involvement, the city's Quakers would reinvent themselves in the twentieth century as champions of world peace and international outreach.

American Friends Service Committee

By the early twentieth century, Philadelphia Quakers abandoned most of the peculiarities of dress and speech that once separated them from the rest of society. No longer did they wear the broad-brimmed hats and scoop bonnets, or the black and drab grey attire of their ancestors. Nor did they use the familiar "thee" and "thou" that distinguished their speech in earlier centuries. Quakers even discarded their longtime avoidance of marrying non-Quakers. Friends no longer considered these practices as being essential to their faith.

Instead, leaders like Rufus Jones (1863–1948) pioneered a new understanding of Quakerism as a mystical religion uniquely suited to the modern age. Jones, a professor of history and philosophy at Haverford College, was probably the most remarkable figure produced by the Society of Friends in the twentieth century. Warm-spirited, quick-witted, and wise, Jones was not only a prolific writer and speaker but also a pivotal figure in reuniting the Hicksites and Orthodox by establishing the American Friends Service Committee (AFSC), a Philadelphia-based organization that works for peace and social justice in the United States and around the world.[1]

The U.S. entry into World War I in 1917 created a conflict of conviction for many Philadelphia Friends. While their historic peace testimony obliged them to remain neutral, many Quakers genuinely believed that they had a moral obligation to stop German atrocities in Europe. In fact, more than two-thirds of the eligible Quaker young men would go on to serve in combat positions during the war. Disciplining or disowning them for their military service was not realistic because a considerable percentage of the older Quaker population supported the war.[2] To address the problem, Jones, along with Henry J. Cadbury (1883–1974), another Haverford professor, organized the AFSC to provide opportunities for conscientious objectors to do relief work in war-torn Europe as an alternative to military service.[3] Stating their desire to provide "a service of love in wartime," Friends offered their services to the United States government "in any constructive work in which they could conscientiously serve humanity."[4] To that end, Jones, the first chairman of AFSC, reached an agreement with the U.S. government and the American Red Cross to create a reconstruction unit that would serve as a vehicle for the young members of peace churches to provide relief work. Quakers, Mennonites, Brethren, and others, who for one reason or another were exempt from the draft, trained at Haverford College and later went to France to join British Friends who would also serve in the unit.[5]

In France, the reconstruction workers were divided into teams. Some helped to operate hospitals and children's homes. Others built shelters for refugees. Still others distributed food, clothing, and bedding for the homeless.[6] Six AFSC workers even managed to gain entry into Russia to help manage the flow of refugees pouring into that country from the west. Together with other American and British workers, these Friends provided emergency food, clothing, and medical care and established refugee camps as well as centers to care for orphaned and abandoned children. When they were advised by the U.S. government in October 1918 to leave Russia because of the revolution, the AFSC workers spent the winter in Omsk, Siberia, where they tried to help Russians who were fleeing Bolshevik forces.[7]

While patriotic fervor spread in the United States encouraged by an elaborate government campaign to stir enthusiasm for the war, intolerance for dissent and intellectual non-conformity grew. Refusing to yield, Cadbury, in an October 1918 letter to the *Philadelphia Public Ledger*, denounced U.S. war policies and the American public's pro-war attitude. His pleas for "moderation" and "fair play"—as well as his hauntingly accurate prediction that "a peace on any other terms will be no peace at all, but the curse of the future"—were received with cries for his dismissal from Haverford College. When he was suspended by the college, Cadbury accepted a position at Andover Theological Seminary, though he continued to work for the AFSC.[8]

During the next few years, Philadelphia Quakers, with Cadbury's enthusiastic support, involved themselves in post-war reconstruction. They went to work in some forty villages located in the Verdun region of France where they supervised the rebuilding of farms, houses, and schools. Purchasing leftover army surplus, including a railroad boxcar full of bayonets, the workers had the supplies melted down and repurposed as farm tools, including metal plows. In so doing, they found an opportunity to literally turn swords into plowshares as advised in the Biblical idiom,

Isaiah 2:4.[9] Nor did the AFSC workers ignore the desperate circumstances of Germany, the country that started the war. Working closely with both the American and French armies, the Quakers were offered German prisoners of war to do the work of reconstruction without pay. Although they accepted the offer, Friends would not exploit German labor. They kept account of every hour the prisoners worked and later traveled to Germany to pay their families the withheld wages, which were desperately needed as that country was suffering from poverty and inflation.[10] Perhaps the greatest of AFSC's undertakings, however, was feeding millions of starving German children after the war.

When three AFSC representatives visited Germany in 1919, they discovered an entire generation of children suffering from the effects of hunger in rickets, poor health, and despair. Shortly after, Herbert Hoover, chairman of the American Relief Administration, requested that the Quakers take charge of distributing food to these malnourished children. AFSC had never addressed relief on such a massive scale, but it rose to meet the challenge.

Kitchens to prepare meals were established across Germany and Austria. By June 1921, Friends were working in 1,640 German communities feeding 1,100,658 children to meet the official government ration of 1,300 calories a day. Those children who needed greater nourishment were given an additional 750 calories per day.[11] These efforts spelled the difference between health, illness, and, in some cases, death for thousands of German children. Nor was the work of AFSC limited to Western Europe.

With the cessation of hostilities, Quaker service teams traveled to the war-ravaged Volga region of Russia where hundreds were dying of starvation and typhus. The poor had become so desperate for food that they were eating the thatch of their cottages, farm animals, birds, and even mice. Friends distributed carloads of grain sent by American church groups, sometimes at the peril of Russian bandits who threatened the supplies. While the Russian Army offered to protect the Quaker service teams, they also wanted to be fed. But Friends refused their demands, insisting that the food must go only to children and nursing mothers. In Poland, Quaker relief workers established an orphanage and assisted in agricultural rehabilitation. After these tasks were completed, the AFSC left behind small international centers in Paris, Berlin, Vienna, Geneva, Warsaw, and Moscow to support nationals who had become interested in improving international relations and world peace. These small centers allowed Friends to monitor the growing turmoil that beset Europe in the 1930s.[12]

In 1934, for example, the Berlin center was overwhelmed by Jews who wanted to escape Hitler's Germany and emigrate to the United States.

After the war, Herbert Hoover, a Quaker from Oregon, was appointed by U.S. President Woodrow Wilson to lead the American Relief Administration, which provided food to millions of starving refugees in Central and Eastern Europe. Unknown artist. (*Library of Congress*)

After World War I, the American Friends Service Committee distributed bread tickets with the illustration of a colonial Quaker to the children of Frankfurt, Germany. (*American Friends Service Committee Collection, Swarthmore College, Swarthmore, PA*)

Henry Cadbury tried to allay their fears by encouraging German Jews to engage with the Nazis to resolve their differences. "Good will, not hate or reprisals, will end, or offset, the evils of the Nazi government's persecution of Jews," he insisted in the June 15, 1934 edition of *The New York Times*.[13] The controversial suggestion, rightfully repudiated by American rabbis, underestimated the depth of German antisemitism and the evils of Hitler's regime.

Cadbury probably realized how naïve his remark was four years later when, on the night of November 9, 1938, Nazi mobs viciously attacked the Jewish communities of Germany, Austria, and the Sudetenland region of Czechoslovakia. For forty-eight hours, Hitler's paramilitary troops—the *Schutzstaffel* and the *Sturmabteilung*—destroyed hundreds of synagogues, desecrated Jewish cemeteries, ransacked and looted some 7,500 Jewish businesses, burnt synagogues, and left shards of glass littering the streets. Known as "*Kristallnacht*," or the "Night of Broken Glass," nearly 100 Jews were killed, and 30,000 Jewish men were arrested and sent to concentration camps.[14]

Jews, whose shops were destroyed and were forbidden to shop in Gentile stores, appealed to the AFSC if they might consider providing food provisions. When Rufus Jones and two other relief workers arrived in Berlin to investigate, Jewish leaders there changed their request and asked that Friends arrange for emigration. The three Quakers requested a meeting with *Reichsführer* Heinrich Himmler to seek permission. Instead, they were received by Reinhard Heydrich, Himmler's subordinate and a high-ranking SS official. After a prolonged discussion, Heydrich granted them permission to implement the emigration program.[15] For the next few years, AFSC focused its complete efforts on the emigration and relocation in America of German Jews. The Berlin center was overwhelmed by desperate Jewish families. Other offices were opened in Rome, Amsterdam, and Vienna to accommodate the growing numbers of refugees. In the United States, the AFSC operated hostels and language camps for the refugees while Quaker meetings across the country sponsored Jewish emigrant families. These efforts continued until U.S. entry into the war in December 1941 forced the workers out of Europe. By that time, some 50,000 refugees had been assisted by Friends.[16]

After World War II, the AFSC engaged in more specialized services: developing small community centers for the dislocated in Germany, France, and Japan; establishing small industries in Finland; and repairing transportation systems in Italy. So vital were these efforts to reconstructing war-torn Europe that the AFSC, along with the British Friends Service Council, received the Nobel Peace Prize on December 10, 1947 for "demonstrating a way of life founded on faith in the victory of spirit over force." Henry Cadbury accepted the honor for the AFSC, appearing at the ceremony in Oslo in a tuxedo he borrowed from the organization's material aids program. "On behalf of the American Friends Service Committee I accept our share of this award with humility and gratitude," Cadbury began his acceptance speech:

We are humble because we recognize what we Quakers of today owe to the generations of Quakers who have for three centuries set the pattern of practical pacifism that we unfalteringly follow. We recognize also that the work of our Committee has been made possible through the cooperation of our fellow prize-winners, the Friends Service Council and by the support in funds, personnel and in sympathetic understanding of thousands of Americans who are not members of our small Society of Friends.

We are grateful that in this award attention is again called to the need for the ideals that we profess—renunciation of all war—practical friendliness across frontiers, reconciliation with former enemies and former friends. Today in America, in Europe and in Asia men need almost as never before to bear an appeal to reason and to patience.

If any should question the appropriateness of bestowing the peace prize upon a group rather than upon an outstanding individual we may say this: The common people of all nations want peace. In the presence of great impersonal forces they feel individually helpless to promote it. You are saying to them here today that common folk, not statesmen, nor generals nor great men of affairs, but just simple plain men and women like the few thousand Quakers and their friends, if they devote themselves to resolute insistence on goodwill in place of force, even in the face of great disaster past or threatened, can do something to build a better, peaceful world. The future hope of peace lies with such personal sacrificial service. To this ideal, humble persons everywhere may contribute.

It is not enough merely for us to do good—feeding and clothing the needy and to receive their heartfelt thanks. We must find ways in which even the needy can share in service. To this end our committee is trying to find means. May I suggest to you and the other countries of Europe a way that you can help us. You will need for this help neither money nor material gifts.

All Europe is rightly anxious about the relations between the United States and the Soviet Union. Here is a place where you can help. Norway, your well loved country, and the other nations of Europe must be the bridge of understanding. You must not take sides with either of us, you must help both of us cooperate. And I know from contacts I have made with persons from many countries of Europe that already they are anxious to do just this. You must have faith to do this—faith in all men, even in Americans and Russians. We earnestly invite you to share in this way our ministry of reconciliation.[17]

After 1947, AFSC played a critical role in the reunification of Philadelphia's Hicksite and Orthodox Friends. The momentum for reconciliation had been building since the beginning of the twentieth century as both groups experienced declines in membership. Reunion became a matter of economy and efficiency. More important, the old theological differences had, for the most part, faded with time and groups had become receptive to liberal theological ideas. Specifically, the idea that the Bible was the product of a particular ancient historical era, and the truth of the theory of the evolution. Hicksite and Orthodox Quakers began to focus more on their mutual—and longstanding—commitment to the peace testimony and social justice. In 1901, for example, they jointly organized a conference for world peace. Women from both yearly meetings also worked together on issues of suffrage and peace. Inspired by the leadership of Alice Paul, a member of Moorestown Friends Meeting, Philadelphia's Quaker women campaigned to pass and ratify the 19th Amendment.[18]

A new generation of Quakers also worked to bridge the gap that once existed between the Hicksites and Orthodox. In 1913, a group of young adult Friends from each branch began to meet regularly to study the separation. The following year, they issued a report to both yearly meetings stating that the separation had not been due so much to differences in religious doctrine as to the issue of authority. The insight prompted both the Orthodox and Hicksite yearly meetings to make significant changes in their disciplining of members. Disownment for marriage to a non-Friend ended and, for the most part, there was no longer an emphasis on plain style of dress or speech. These earlier efforts paved the way, in 1917, for members of both branches to organize the AFSC as a means of providing service opportunities for conscientious objectors in World War I. Among the opportunities for alternative service were providing food to starving miners in labor disputes in Appalachia, assisting the Red Cross in their battlefield ambulance units during the war and helping to rebuild Europe after the war.

Other collaborations between Philadelphia's Orthodox and Hicksite Friends followed including the establishment of Pendle Hill, a Quaker retreat and study center in 1930, the Friends Council on Education (1932), and the Friends Committee on National Legislation (1943). These organizations, particularly the AFSC, served to unify Friends and to develop several Quaker leaders, including Douglas and Dorothy

Steere, Howard and Anna Brinton, Rufus Jones, and Henry Cadbury, who influenced Philadelphia Yearly Meeting Friends for decades to come. Collectively, the leadership of these Friends enabled the Peace Committees and Religious Life Committees of the two Philadelphia Yearly Meetings to merge and to permit the formation of monthly meetings with membership in both Orthodox and Hicksite Yearly Meetings.[19]

In 1946, the yearly meetings agreed to establish a Philadelphia General Meeting which would be held in the autumn and be attended by both Orthodox and Hicksite Friends, though separate sessions would continue to be held in the spring. Four years later, in 1950, a committee was formed with representatives from both yearly meetings to prepare a common book of discipline. Titled *Faith and Practice*, the book was published in 1955, the same year a unified Philadelphia Yearly Meeting convened at Arch Street Meeting House, ending a schism that had lasted for 128 years.[20]

After reunification, the AFSC continued to act on and expand its original mission to work for peace and social justice in the United States and around the world. Believing that peace can no longer be defined as the absence of organized violence and the relief of human suffering, the Service Committee became more involved in the struggle for human rights and social justice in developing nations where the disparity between rich and poor is a primary cause of illiteracy, poverty, and war. To that end, AFSC established community development projects in Africa, Latin America, the Middle East, and Southeast Asia while also working for peace in these regions. In 1966, for example, Friends administered programs of childcare and prosthetics for war-injured Vietnam civilian refugees and their children and a year later sent medical supplies to North Vietnam on the ship *Phoenix*. Other projects included protesting apartheid in South Africa, the establishment of a major health clinic in Haiti and advising farmers in North Korea on how to increase food production sustainably in the 1990s.

In a related effort to lessen global tensions, the AFSC brought together mid-career diplomats from many nations in informal conferences to discuss ways to prevent conflicts from developing. These conferences now take place in Europe, Africa, India, all parts of Asia, Washington, D.C., and at the United Nations, and include young leaders and professionals as well as diplomats. Because of these efforts, the AFSC established a global reputation for advocating nonviolent resolution of international conflicts.[21] At the same time, the Service Committee has been concerned with eliminating injustice at home.

In the United States, the AFSC has become a powerful advocate for African Americans, Mexican Americans, migrant workers, Native American, and the poor. Their goal is to help these groups to organize themselves for community action and thus obtain the better schools, housing, and working conditions they deserve. Quaker efforts began in the mid-1950s with the emergence of the modern civil rights movement and the publication of a 1955 AFSC-sponsored pamphlet titled *Speaking Truth to Power*. Co-authored by Bayard Rustin (1912–1987), the pamphlet promoted the non-violent resolution of conflict inspired by Mahatma Gandhi, the Indian revolutionary who employed non-violent resistance to lead the successful campaign for India's independence from British rule.[22]

Rustin, an African American Quaker from West Chester, was a prominent civil rights leader and the chief organizer of the August 1963 March on Washington for Jobs and Freedom. He served as the primary liaison for the AFSC and the Reverend Dr. Martin Luther King Jr. on his visit to India in 1959 to help strengthen the nonviolent African American civil rights movement.[23] The AFSC later published King's 1963 *Letter from Birmingham Jail* as a stand-alone pamphlet. These activities inspired PYM to undertake a community development project in Chester, Pennsylvania, and to establish the Minorities Economic Development Fund to finance similar projects around Philadelphia.[24]

Philadelphia Quakers have long been champions of human rights for other minority groups as well. In 1973, for example, PYM publicly voiced its support for gay rights, and by 1991, it was publishing a guide for same-sex couples that wanted to be married in Quaker ceremonies. AFSC also directed volunteer efforts to address domestic poverty in farm labor camps, mining communities, on Indian reservations, and on the streets of inner cities, as well as opposed solitary confinement in the criminal justice system and provided legal services for those who wanted to immigrate to the United States.[25]

Today, the AFSC continues these humanitarian activities while also raising public awareness on the issues of war and peace. The committee works to inform Americans against the dangers of increasing militarism and the status of the U.S. military-industrial complex via speaking tours, the publication of literature, a campaign to end the draft, and participation in demonstrations and protests sponsored by other peace and social justice groups. Not only is the AFSC directed by a genuine spirit of love towards others in all these efforts, but also provides the kind of moral leadership we all keep hoping to find in our contemporary society.

Whiter Philadelphia Quakerism?

Since the eighteenth century, when Quakers comprised a substantial percentage of the city's population, PYM has witnessed a steady decline in membership. Statistics from 2020 indicated that PYM then had 10,053 members spread across the Philadelphia region among 106 monthly meetings, a precipitous drop from more than 30,000 members in 1775 or even the 15,000 recorded members in 1925.[1] Since 2020, several monthly meetings have fewer than ten attenders at their weekly meeting for worship and not much more than fifty on their membership rolls.

PYM also faces a leadership problem due, in part, to the aging of those members who possess a firm understanding of Quaker faith, history, and practice and were once active in the outreach programs and schools established by Friends. This population became substantially older during the late twentieth and early twenty-first centuries and are now in their mid-to-late '80s and '90s.[2] Today, many of those elderly Friends reside in retirement communities and few are as active as they once were in their monthly meetings. In fact, the building and operation of retirement communities has become a major form of outreach for PYM.

These patterns raise serious questions about the future of Philadelphia Quakerism. Can today's Friends continue to exercise as meaningful an influence on the City of Brotherly Love as did their ancestors? Are there enough young Friends who are willing to assume responsibility for the leadership of not only the yearly meeting, but also of outreach programs and Quaker schools and colleges? If not, will Philadelphia Yearly Meeting survive?

If PYM made an active and concerted effort to attract others to the Quaker faith, it might be able to replenish the leadership void within their own ranks. Unlike Friends who belong to the pastoral and evangelical branches of Quakerism, however, Philadelphia Quakers do not proselytize believing that others should feel led to become "convinced" without any outward coercion. Lacking experienced leaders, PYM, over the last half century, has surrendered the responsibilities for their institutions to non-Quakers, or Friends who place a greater emphasis on inclusiveness rather than on the theology, social testimonies, and discipline that once made Quakers a people among peoples.

To be sure, leadership has always been problematic for Quakers. Historically, Friends have demonstrated collective—not individual—leadership. While an individual concern may inspire the group to act on a particular cause, Quakers rely on consensus decision-making to move forward on that cause and do so as a group. Thus, Friends tend to express ambivalence about anything that suggests an unequal distribution of power and authority in PYM and its constituent quarterly and monthly meetings.

At the same time, there is a distinctive Quaker leadership style that can be best described as "servant leadership." In this model, the leader's primary responsibility is to serve others. He is not the initiator, but rather a responder to the Light, or Divine Will. The servant leader possesses a gift for listening carefully to the concerns of the group. He enables others to reach consensus in the decision-making process by accurately articulating the sense of the group. These special abilities enable the servant leader to organize the group to act by setting goals and channeling the energy of members to proceed in a mutually agreeable direction that will make life better for themselves and/or others who are being served.[3]

This kind of leadership not only requires special abilities, but also experience acquired within the monthly meeting over time as well as a firm understanding of Quaker faith, history, and practice. The numbers of these servant leaders are dwindling among Philadelphia Quakers because membership within PYM today tends to be open to anyone who is sympathetic with the Quaker values of diversity and pacifism and is comfortable with the worship and business practices of the local meeting they join. Today's members do not need to possess a functional understanding of the theology upon which the faith was founded, the history of the denomination, or the discipline which brings moral integrity to it. Nor do they even need to be Christian.

Today, Philadelphia Quakers seem to have forgotten the historical fact that their faith was founded as a Christian religion rooted in the New Testament Gospel of John. Early Friends believed that they were taking Christianity back to its most basic form free of the rituals and ordained ministry of the Anglican and Catholic churches. In fact, William Penn argued that Quakerism was best understood as *"primitive Christianity* revived."[4] Over the centuries, however, Friends' rejection of firm religious dogma resulted in a diversity of thought on the subject. As a result, there are some members of Philadelphia Yearly Meeting who hew to Christian tradition,

A satiric look at the unprogrammed ministry among Philadelphia Quakers today. (*Signe Wilkinson*)

but many others who embrace a universalist perspective, and still others who are agnostic. PYM's leadership not only accepts this kind of theological diversity but celebrates it as a sign of inclusiveness within its religious body.

What happens when inclusiveness overwhelms the religious foundations upon which Quakerism was founded? Can PYM continue to grow if not survive as a church if it defines itself strictly by the ecumenical values of simplicity, peace, integrity, community, and equality?

The American Friends Service Committee appears to believe that it cannot only survive but continue to flourish. While Philadelphia remains the organization's headquarters, the AFSC has become a majority non-Quaker organization. Today, most of the staff are not Friends and most of the organization's donations and money come from non-Quakers impressed by its idealism and past achievements. However, some Friends who left the AFSC believe that beginning in the 1960s the organization made dangerous compromises with the larger society and no longer maintained a strong peace witness.[5]

An argument can be made that the AFSC, like any organization that works for social justice and peace, benefits from inclusion because it brings greater diversity of ideas, advances peace theory, and produces more broad-based action making their efforts more effective in preventing future wars and in building a more peaceful global community. But there are other churches who are firmly wedded to their faith community and have achieved even greater success than AFSC in their activism.

Since the 1980s, the Catholic Church has taken the lead in the international peace movement among all other religious groups. The driving force of the movement is Pax Christi International in which laypeople, bishops, and other religious members work as equals in 120 member organizations worldwide. As a faith-based Catholic movement, Pax Christi's efforts to resolve conflicts are informed by a deep understanding of religion. The organization is more than twice as likely to achieve their goals than similar organizations because of its strong faith-based connections to communities and institutional ties to governments, which enables the church to play a key role in mediation. While Catholic activists are not always comfortable identifying with the institutional church, many still attend Mass, belong to intentional faith communities, and are inspired in their work by their Catholic beliefs and values. They also feel comfortable collaborating with other religious groups because they are firmly rooted in their Catholic faith.[6] The AFSC might find that they, too, would be more successful in their outreach programs if they followed such a model of faith-based activism rather than delegating leadership to non-Quakers. A similar problem exists among Philadelphia's Friends schools and colleges.

In the twentieth century, Philadelphia's Quakers have had no greater form of outreach than the thirty-eight Friends schools and three colleges they established. Many of the graduates went on in their lives to assume positions of leadership in society.[7] Today, however, the Quaker enrollments of these schools and colleges are less than 5 percent with even fewer Quaker faculty and administrators. Annual tuitions range from an average of $20,000 for elementary schools to $45,000 for high schools to $70,000 for boarding schools, making it impossible for Friends, many of whom work in non-profits, to send their children to those schools and colleges even with scholarship assistance.[8]

Most of the Friends schools have also divorced themselves from the monthly meetings who established them. Instead, those schools have incorporated themselves and established boards of trustees, many of whom are non-Friends and who emphasize the necessity of bigger and better facilities to compete with other private schools.

Nor is there much effort to teach students about Quakerism. While all the Friends schools still hold a weekly meeting for worship and operate community service programs, few require students to take a course on Quakerism if one exists at all. As a result, students tend to gain an understanding of Quaker faith, history, and practice through osmosis. The K-12 schools in particular have compromised their Quaker mission for greater success in the market competition that drives independent education. Their trustees, both Quaker and non-Quaker, have become enamored with building more modern facilities, bigger enrollments, winning athletic teams, and increasing matriculation rates to the Ivy League. None of those things have as much of an impact on the quality of the education at Friends schools as the faculty who teach there.[9]

To be sure, Friends schools and colleges are not immune to the economic patterns of society. Like all private educational institutions, they are forced to operate like businesses, competing for the same students, generating public exposure to raise funds, and finding ways to cut costs while simultaneously improving the quality of education they provide. The danger is falling victim to these pressures. Nor is there anything new about the market mentality.

Historian Frederick Tolles reminds us that the Quakers who established Philadelphia's first Friends schools in the late seventeenth century had an impeccable reputation as honest businessmen which enabled them to accumulate significant wealth. In the process, their once uncompromising commitment to faith yielded to remarkable financial success. What was once a mutual interaction between religion and everyday life became a conflict between the Meeting House and the Counting House. By the 1750s, the Quaker merchants who established those schools had allowed their spiritual integrity to be compromised by their enjoyment of riches and worldly place. As a result, they established schools with different missions. There was a Latin school catering to students who would go on to become professionals, and English schools to prepare students for a successful career in business.

Even in their outreach the wealthy Quaker merchants who oversaw the Friends schools tended to vacillate between the original mission of those schools, which focused on a practical education for all of Philadelphia's children, and a classical curriculum in preparation for higher education and social mobility. Some Quaker educational reformers like Roberts

Vaux, Daniel Smith, and Thomas Scattergood founded charity schools for free blacks and the poor in the late eighteenth century and in the early nineteenth century helped to establish Philadelphia's public schools by creating an inexpensive way to educate mass numbers of poor children.[10] While the intentions of Vaux, Smith, and Scattergood may have been based on the moral uplift of the poor, some historians have accused them of using education as a means of social control, or engaging in the insidious design of keeping the children of the poor and working classes in purposeful subordination. In so doing, these Quakers reformers, who were also market capitalists, hoped to perpetuate the labor force of their factories by creating another generation of wage slaves.[11]

Other Quaker educators like Richard Mott Jones and Richard Gummere believed that the more affluent members of society had a special responsibility for social and political leadership and that they should receive an elite education to prepare for it. That education was based on a competitive ethic that was cultivated in the classroom, as well as on the playing fields that surrounded their new country day school in 1925. Their philosophy formed the college preparatory mission of the modern-day William Penn Charter School.[12]

Should these individuals be condemned for using education as a vehicle for social control of the poor and greater economic and social opportunity for the wealthy? Not necessarily. But their actions, no matter how willing or unwitting, established an on-going tension for Quaker education. In other words, should Friends schools and colleges strive to be "all things for all people" or more selective institutions that cater to the best and brightest regardless of their religious denomination. While this tension represents an issue of vision, the process taken has often become a moral issue. Not only does the process require a willingness to listen carefully to the ideas of all concerned parties, but an openness to admit mistakes as well as to take responsibility for them. Just as important, the process requires working together with all parties to achieve a quality consensus, rather than compromising on the path of least resistance. The degree to which that process is respected has a tremendous impact on the moral integrity of our Friends schools and colleges as well as the academic reputations they enjoy.

How can today's Friends in good conscience abandon this responsibility for the schools and colleges they themselves created by allowing non-Quakers to assume leadership for them? Non-Friends who dominate the ranks of the administration and faculty may very well be dedicated individuals who try their best to act on Quaker principles amidst the pressures of educational consumerism and the market mentality that has gripped our schools and colleges. But there is no substitute for those who have made a genuine commitment to the Quaker faith. They are the ones who should have a functional understanding of Quaker decision-making as well as a vision of education that is consistent with Quaker faith, history, and practice.

I do not mean to suggest that the only good educators are Quaker, or that Friends schools should return to the religiously guarded days of the eighteenth-century. But I cannot deny that my own experience in Friends education was as meaningful as it was because the schools and college that I attended in the 1960s and 1970s employed a critical mass of Quakers in leadership positions and that today's Friends schools and colleges have lost a great deal of Quaker influence because Friends have abandoned their responsibilities to those institutions. Instead of addressing the problem, so many Quakers seem more content to allow non-Friends to run their schools while they complain about the high cost of a Quaker education and the need to support public schools or other forms of outreach. Creating a critical mass of Quakers in Friends schools and colleges is only part of the solution, though.

If Quaker institutions must compete in the wider market of independent education, they should be searching for ways to preserve the integrity of their mission by returning to their Quaker roots. Instead of following the "bigger is better" mentality of other educational institutions by building newer facilities, expanding curricular offerings, emphasizing academic success rather than learning, and focusing on student matriculation rates to select colleges or graduate schools, Friends should return to the time-tested fundamentals that have always distinguished a Quaker education. Age-appropriate learning, integrating community service into the curriculum, conflict resolution programs, experiential education, and interdisciplinary and multiple intelligence learning were all staples of Quaker education three centuries before they were in vogue at any other private school or college.

PYM is at an important crossroad. It can either choose to assume greater responsibility for their church, their outreach programs and their schools and colleges, or continue to defer that responsibility to other non-Friends who, however well-intentioned, have little to no understanding of the faith, history, or practice that informed those institutions. If PYM chooses the latter course, it will be extremely difficult to survive as a religious body or to do justice to the meaningful contributions earlier generations of Friends made to the city. Ultimately the decision is theirs to make. If Friends fail, they will have nobody but themselves to blame.

Endnotes

Chapter 1

1 W. Braithwaite, *The Beginnings of Quakerism* (London: Macmillan, 1912), pp. 1-2, 12, 22-27.

2 C. Hill, *The World Turned Upside Down. Radical Ideas During the English Revolution* (New York: Penguin Books, 1985), pp. 14-15.

3 H. Barbour, *The Quakers in Puritan England* (New Haven, CT: Yale University, 1964), pp. 24-32.

4 H. Ingle, *First Among Friends: George Fox & the Creation of Quakerism* (New York: Oxford University Press, 1994), 18-23.

5 G. Fox, *Journal*, edited by J. Nickalls. (Philadelphia: Philadelphia Yearly Meeting, 1985), pp. 7-8. Fox's journal was originally published in 1694, three years after his death and after editing by Thomas Ellwood. Considered a classic of religious literature, the journal was not written contemporaneously to the events it describes, but rather compiled many years later.

    While most of the journal was dictated to Ellwood by Fox himself, other parts were constructed from diverse sources and written as if by him by later editors including Norman Penney (1911, 1924) and Jack Nickalls (1952).

    Fox was careful not to discuss dissent within the Quaker movement. Nor does he emphasize the contributions of others to the development of Quakerism. Instead, Fox portrays himself as always in the right and always vindicated by God's interventions on his behalf. [H. Ingle, *op. cit.*, pp. 250-52].

6 Fox, *op. cit.*, p. 11.

7 *Ibid.*, pp. 12, 16, 34.

8 *Ibid.*, pp. 143-45, 159.

9 *Ibid.*, pp. 263.

10 H. Brinton, *Friends for 300 Years: The History and beliefs of the Society of Friends since George Fox started the Quaker movement* (Wallingford, PA: Pendle Hill, 1976, 5th edition), pp. 59-82; and D. Johns, "Quaker Theology and Spirituality: Worship and Sacraments," in *The Oxford Handbook of Quaker Studies*, edited by S. Angell and P. Dandelion. (New York: Oxford University, 2013), pp. 261-64.

11 Fox, *op. cit.*, pp. 103-104; and Ingle, *op. cit.*, p. 81. When Fox began to preach publicly in 1647, he seemed to have had no desire to establish a religious sect;

only to proclaim what he considered the pure and most basic principles of Christianity. But when Fox felt called to climb Pendle Hill in 1652 and had a vision of many like-minded people seeking Christ, he became determined to establish a sect of his own.

12 H. Barbour and J. Frost, *The Quakers* Westport, CT: Greenwood Press, 1988), pp. 11, 29.

13 E. Vipont, *George Fox and the Valiant Sixty* (London: Hamish Hamilton, 1975), pp. iii-vii.

14 Barbour, *op. cit.*, pp. 160-80. When referring to the social testimonies established by the early Friends, contemporary Philadelphia Quakers employ the acronym, SPICE: Simplicity, Peace, Integrity, Community and Equality. [Philadelphia Yearly Meeting, "Concerns, Leadings and Testimonies," *Faith and Practice* (Philadelphia: Religious Society of Friends, 2017) www.pym. org/faith-and-practice/faith-reflected-practice-daily-life/concerns-leadings-testimonies/ Retrieved, February 20, 2023]. The American Friends Service Committee adds a sixth testimony, which is Stewardship. [See E. Clarke, *et. al.*, *An Introduction to Quaker Testimonies.* (Philadelphia: American Friends Service Committee, 2011)].

15 Fox, *op. cit.*, p. 58. On another occasion, Fox gave equal credit for the nickname "Quaker" to Nathanael Barton, a Presbyterian preacher in Derby, who signed a complaint against him for preaching his nonconformist religious beliefs in public. [G. Fox, *Cain against Abel, Representing New England's Church Hierarchy in Opposition to Her Christian Protestant Dissenters* (London: no publisher, 1675), p. 27].

16 Fox, *op. cit.*, p. 65.

17 P. Brock, *The Quaker Peace Testimony, 1660–1914* (York, England: Sessions Book Trust, 1990), pp. 9-23; and Hill, *op. cit.*, pp. 241-42. Both Brock and Hill point out that several of the early Quaker leaders had once been soldiers in Cromwell's Army including, James Nayler, William Dewsbury, Richard Hubberthorne, and Edward Burrough. In fact, Fox himself wavered on the issue of pacifism until 1660 when it became necessary to demonstrate that Quakers were not conspiring to overthrow the newly restored Stuart monarchy.

18 G. Fox, "A Declaration from the Harmless & Innocent People of God Called Quakers to Charles II, 1660–1661," quoted in Fox, *op. cit.*, p. 234.

19 R. Allen, "Restoration Quakerism, 1660-1691," in Angell and Dandelion, *op. cit.*, pp. 30-34.

20 Hill, *op. cit.*, pp. 248-51.

21 Fox, *op. cit.*, pp. 71-72.

22 A. Murphy, *William Penn. A Life* (New York: Oxford University Press, 2019), pp. 12-17, 23-28. There is no evidence of Penn's expulsion in the records of Christ Church. Penn, himself, used the word "banished" when he referred to his departure from the college. [Letter, J. Frost to author, Philadelphia, March 3, 2023].

23 S. Pepys, *Diary*, entry for April 22, 1661. www.pepysdiary.com, retrieved February 21, 2023.

24 Murphy, *op. cit.*, pp. 29-31. Calvinism was the established church in Holland at this time, but Jews, Anabaptists, and even Catholics could worship freely.

25 *Ibid.*, pp. 37-38.

26 Pepys, *op. cit.*, entry for August 30, 1664.

27 Murphy, *op. cit.*, pp. 39-40, 49. According to J. William Frost, another Penn biographer, "there is no portrait of William Penn drawn from life." The portrait of a young William Penn in armor at the Historical Society of Pennsylvania in Philadelphia is a nineteenth-century copy. Since that portrait

bears the motto of Oliver Cromwell, it is most likely a likeness of Sir William Penn. [Letter, Frost to author].

28 Murphy, *op. cit.*, pp. 39-40.

29 W. Penn, "An Account of the Convincement of William Penn Delivered by Himself to Thomas Harvey," (1677) *Journal of Friends Historical Society*, Vol. 32, pp. 23-23 (Philadelphia: Friends Historical Society, 1935). The best source on the evolution of Penn's religious thought is M. Endy, *William Penn and Early Quakerism* (Princeton, NJ: Princeton University Press, 1973).

30 Murphy, *op. cit.*, pp. 53-55.

31 H. Wildes, *William Penn: A Biography* (New York: Macmillan, 1974), p. 46. After diligently searching for primary source documentation on the sword story, Quaker historian Henry J. Cadbury could find no record of it prior to 1852. [J. Frost, "'Wear the Sword As Long As Thou Canst': William Penn in Myth and History." *Explorations* in *American Culture*, Vol. 4, *pp. 21-22* (Philadelphia: University of Pennsylvania Press, *2000*).

32 Murphy, *op. cit.*, p. 54. Joseph Besse, Penn's first biographer, suggests that the recently converted Quaker was summarily dismissed from his father's household and reduced to poverty. [J. Besse, editor. *A Collection of the Works of William Penn* (2 vols. London, 1726), Vol. I: 4]. However, Penn's most recent biographer suggests that the banishment may have been only temporary. [Murphy, *op. cit.*, p. 54].

33 E. Bronner and D. Fraser, *William Penn's Published Writings, 1660–1726. An Interpretive Bibliography* (Philadelphia: University of Pennsylvania, 1986), pp. 96-99. Hugh Barbour argues that Penn's early writings are more reflective of a an intellectual and debater than a theologian. Penn's experience, according to Barbour, "was in ethics; not worship." Thus, Penn never became the Society of Friends' theological leader. That distinction belongs to Robert Barclay, whose *Apology* (1676) is still considered the definitive Quaker doctrinal book due to Barclay's powerful articulation of Quaker worship. [See: H. Barbour, "The Young Controversialist," in *The World of William Penn*, edited by R. Dunn and M. Dunn, editors, (Philadelphia: University of Pennsylvania Press, 1986), pp. 15-29].

34 Bronner and Fraser, *op. cit.*, pp. 102-104.

35 *Ibid.*, pp. 112-17.

36 M. Dunn, *William Penn: Politics and Conscience* (Princeton, NJ: Princeton University Press, 1967), 13-16. By preaching on Gracechurch Street in London, Penn violated the recently passed Conventicle Act forbidding nonconformist religious gatherings of more than five people. During the subsequent trial, Penn challenged the legality of the indictment and refused to plead without seeing a written copy. Since this was not given, he pleaded not guilty. When the jury found Penn guilty of "speaking in the street," but refused to add the words "in an unlawful assembly," the magistrates ordered the jurors to be jailed without food or water until they reached a guilty verdict. Penn called to them not to give up their rights as Englishmen. Two months later, when the jurors were released on a writ of *habeas corpus*, they sued the mayor and recorder, winning their case before the Court of Common Pleas.

37 Murphy, *op. cit.*, pp. 92-93.

38 *Ibid.*, p. 80.

39 Barbour and Frost, *op. cit.*, pp. 65-68.

40 D. Fischer, *Albion's Seed: Four British Folkways on America* (New York: Oxford University Press, 1991 paperback edition), pp. 419-455.

41 J. Soderlund, *Lenape Country: Delaware Valley Society Before William Penn* (Philadelphia: University of Pennsylvania Press, 2015), pp. 48-63; and Murphy, *op. cit.*, pp. 114-119.

42 E. Bronner, *William Penn's "Holy Experiment." The Founding of Pennsylvania,
    1681–1701* (Westport, CT: Greenwood Press, 1978), pp. 22-23.

43 J. Trussell, *William Penn: Architect of a Nation* (Harrisburg: Pennsylvania
    Historical and Museum Commission, 1983), p. 27.

44 Bronner, *op. cit.*, p. 25.

45 W. Penn, "The Frame of Government and Laws as Agreed Upon in England,"
    May 5, 1682 in R. Dunn and M. Dunn, editors, *The Papers of William Penn.* (5
    vols., Philadelphia: University of Pennsylvania Press, 1982), Vol. II, pp. 222-27.

46 Letter, William Penn to James Harrison, March 5, 1681, quoted in Dunn and Dunn,
    (1982) *op. cit.*, II, pp. 107-9. James Harrison was a Quaker minister from Northern
    England who helped to promote settlement in Pennsylvania. In this letter, Penn
    commissioned Harrison as one of his land agents. But the letter is more significant
    because it is the only reference Penn ever made to his New World Colony as a
    "Holy Experiment." The term captured not only Penn's religious vision for his
    colony, but also his desire to experiment with democracy and social diversity.

Chapter 2

1   Bronner, *op. cit.*, p. 31.

2   For passenger names, religious affiliations, and occupations, see: Walter L.
    Sheppard, editor, *William Penn's Colony: Passengers and Ships, Prior to 1684*
    (Baltimore: Genealogical Publishing Company, 1970).

3   For ship dimensions, see: G. Vaux, "The Embarkation, Voyage and Arrival of
    the Ship 'Welcome,' 1682," in *Bulletin of the Friends Historical Association*, Vol.
    21, No. 2 (Philadelphia: Friends Historical Association, Autumn 1932), p. 59.

4   For passenger and crew diet, smallpox epidemic and weather conditions, see:
    Wildes, *op. cit.*, pp. 165-66.

5   Ship and passenger estimates were made by William Penn, who recorded the
    arrival of "about ninety ships," each carrying about eighty passengers, or a total
    of 7,200 immigrants from 1682 to 1685. [W. Penn, "A Further Account of the
    Province of Pennsylvania," in A. Myers, editor, *Narratives of Early Pennsylvania,
    West New Jersey and Delaware, 1630–1707* (New York: Charles Scribner's
    Sons, 1912), p. 260].

6   *Ibid.*, pp. 264-65.

7   J. Illick, *Colonial Pennsylvania: A History* (New York: Charles Scribners' Sons,
    1976), pp. 22-30; and J. Soderlund, editor, *William Penn and the founding of
    Pennsylvania, 1680–1684: A Documentary History* (Philadelphia: University of
    Pennsylvania Press, 1983), p. 81.

8   Murphy, *op. cit.*, pp. 148, 155

9   Murphy, *op. cit.*, pp. 148, 158.

10 Bronner, *op. cit.*, pp. 1-2, 14-15.

11 Frost, (2000), *op. cit.*, pp. *15-18.* Frost argues that Penn's use of the term
    "experiment" referred to a "sign of grace." He supports his contention by
    pointing to two letters Penn wrote in 1681 to prospective colonists—James
    Harrison and Robert Turner—both of which refer to his colony as "an example
    to be set up to the nations." [See: Dunn & Dunn, (1982), *op. cit.*, II, pp. 106,
    110]. The phrase is a scriptural reference to Isaiah 11:10, according to Frost,
    and indicates that "Penn saw his receiving the charter as a testament of God's
    providential gift and as a sign of the approach of the millennium."

12 Murphy, *op. cit.*, p. 148; Bronner, *op. cit.*, p. 6; J. Illick, *William Penn the
    Politician* (Ithaca, New York: Cornell University Press, 1965), p. 40. Murphy,

Bronner and Illick, among other historians, view Penn's establishment of a New World colony as an "experiment" in the modern sense of the term with religious toleration and self-government among other things.

13 Bronner, *op. cit.*, p. 6; and Endy, *op. cit.*, pp. 348-49.

14 Bronner and Fraser, *op. cit.*, p. 96.

15 M. Dunn, *op. cit.*, pp. 10, 44-47.

16 Fischer, *op. cit.*, pp. 420-38.

17 M. Zuckerman, *Peaceable Kingdoms: New England Towns in the Eighteenth Century* (New York: Alfred A. Knopf, 1970), pp. 50-51, 57-58.

18 *Ibid.*, pp. 61-64. Zuckerman later argued that Quaker-founded Pennsylvania in its political, economic, social, and religious development provided the pattern for the rest of America much more than Puritan New England. [See: Zuckerman, *Friends and Neighbors: Group Life in America's First Plural Society* (Philadelphia: Temple University Press, 1982), pp. 3-25.

19 J. Krugler, *English and Catholic: The Lords Baltimore in the Seventeenth Century* (Baltimore: Johns Hopkins University Press, 2004), pp. 169-208, 250-67.

20 D. Boorstin, *The Americans: The Colonial Experience* (New York: Random House, 1958), pp. 105-9, 123-38.

21 J. Frost, *A Perfect Freedom: Religious Liberty in Pennsylvania* (University Park, PA: Penn State Press, 1990), pp. 12, 21, 65. Restrictive measures against Jews and Muslims continued after 1701 when Penn issued a new constitution called the Charter of Liberties, even though it included a provision for the liberty of conscience to all who believed in God. [Penn, "Charter of Privileges," (1701) in Dunn & Dunn (1982), *op. cit.*, IV, p. 106].

22 Bronner, *op. cit.*, p. 27; and Trussell, *op. cit.*, pp. 30-31.

23 W. Penn, "Frame of Government," (1682) in Dunn & Dunn (1982), *op. cit.*, II, pp. 222-27.

24 W. Penn, "Preface to First Frame of Government," (1682) in Dunn & Dunn, (1982), *op. cit.*, II, p. 212.

25 Penn, "Frame of Government," (1682) in Dunn & Dunn (1982), II, pp. 213-27.

26 W. Penn, "Second Frame of Government," April 2, 1683, in J. Soderlund, *William Penn and the Founding of Pennsylvania, 1680–1684: A Documentary History* (Philadelphia: University of Pennsylvania Press, 1983), pp. 265-73.

27 A. Mekeel, "The Founding Years, 1681–1789," in *Friends in the Delaware Valley: Philadelphia Yearly Meeting, 1681–1981*, edited by J. Moore. (Haverford, PA: Friends Historical Association, 1981), pp. 23-24.

28 Frost (1990), *op. cit.*, pp. iii-iv; and Murphy, *op. cit.*, pp. 365-66.

29 J. Soderlund, *Lenape Country: Delaware Valley Society Before William Penn* (Philadelphia: University of Pennsylvania Press, 2016), pp. 2-11.

30 W. Penn, *William Penn's Own Account of the Lenni Lenape or Delaware Indians*, (1683), edited by A. Myers. (Wallingford, PA: Middle Atlantic Press, 1970), p. 41.

31 Letter, William Penn to Pennsylvania Indians, London, England: October 18, 1681 quoted in *ibid.*, p. 60.

32 Bronner, *op. cit.*, p. 63.

33 Bronner, *op. cit.*, pp. 63-64. The treaty between Penn and the Lenni Lenape supposedly took place at the Indian village of Shackamaxon, now the Kensington neighborhood of Philadelphia. However, there is no documentary evidence to support the so-called "Great Treaty" that has been mythologized by Voltaire and Benjamin West's 1771 anachronistic painting of the event. [F. Jennings, "Brother Miquon: Good Lord!" in Dunn & Dunn (1986), *op. cit.*, p.198].

34 C. Weslager, *The Delaware Indians*. (New Brunswick, NJ: Rutgers University Press, 2000), pp. 157-58. Jean Soderlund shows that in contrast to Pennsylvania's policy of fair dealing with the Lenni Lenape, the Quakers who settled West New Jersey in the 1670s sought to acquire as much Lenape territory as possible for their own use and to sell as real estate to other white settlers. Taking advantage of the epidemics that ravaged Lenape communities and introducing slavery to the colony, West New Jersey Quakers treated the Indians as poorly as the Puritans in New England and the Anglicans who settled the Chesapeake region. [Soderlund (2022)].

35 Penn (1683), *op. cit.*, pp. 33-34.

36 Murphy, *op. cit.*, pp. 184-86, 268-69. Interestingly, Penn, in a 1701 will, did "give [his] blacks their freedom" and bequeathed "one-hundred acres to Old Sam," his favorite slave. [See: Penn, "Last Will and Testament, October 30, 1701," in Dunn & Dunn (1982), *op. cit.*, IV, pp. 112-15.

37 Francis Pastorius, "Germantown Protest Against Slavery," (1688), quoted in *Pennsylvania History: Essays and Documents*, edited by Jeffrey A. Davis & Paul D. Newman. (New York: Prentice Hall, 2010), 56-57.

38 Katherine Gerbner, "'We Are Against the Traffik of Men-Body': The Germantown Quaker Protest of 1688 and the Origins of American Abolitionism," *Pennsylvania History*. Vol. 74, No. 2 (Spring 2007): 149-172.

39 Bronner, *op. cit.*, p. 31; and Murphy, *op. cit.*, p. 148.

40 Trussell, *op. cit.*, pp. 31-32.

41 Penn, "A Short Advertisement upon the Situation and Extent of the City of Philadelphia and the ensuing Platform thereof, by the Surveyor-General," (1683) in Dunn & Dunn, (1982), *op. cit.*, II, pp. 458-60. Penn attached document to an August 16, 1683 letter Penn sent to the Free Society of Traders along with a copy of a map of the city drafted by his Surveyor-General Thomas Holme.

42 B. Bailyn, *Education in the Forming of American Society* (New York: W.W. Norton, 1972).

43 Penn, Letter to Gulielma Penn and Children, August 4, 1682, in Dunn & Dunn (1982), *op. cit.*, II, p. 271.

44 Penn, "Frame of Government," (1682) in Dunn & Dunn (1982), *op. cit.*, II: 216.

45 Penn, "Preface to frame of Government," (1682) in Dunn & Dunn (1982), *op. cit.*, II, p. 214.

46 W. Kashatus, *A Virtuous Education: William Penn's Vision for Philadelphia Schools* (Wallingford, PA: Pendle Hill Press, 1997), pp. 39-40.

47 E. Bronner, *"Village into Town, 1701–1746,"* in *Philadelphia: A 300-Year History*, edited by Russell F. Weigley. (New York: W.W. Norton & Company, 1982), pp. 43-52.

48 *Ibid.*, pp. 44-45.

49 Murphy, *op. cit.*, pp. 164-66, 225, 232-35, 352-55.

50 J. Frost, *The Keithian Controversy in Early Pennsylvania* (Norwood, PA: Norwood Editions, 1980).

51 Murphy, *op. cit.*, pp. 252-53, 275-79.

52 Bronner (1978), *op. cit.*, pp. 246-249.

53 G. Nash, *The Liberty Bell* (New Haven, CT: Yale University Press, 2010), pp. 1-5. In 1751, Isaac Norris, the Speaker of the Pennsylvania Assembly ordered a bell to be cast at London's Whitechapel Foundry to serve the City of Philadelphia as a means of communication, gathering citizens for celebration, mourning or for the news of the day. Norris also viewed the bell as a way to celebrate fifty years of peace, prosperity and religious toleration as guaranteed by William Penn's 1701 Charter of Privileges.

In September 1752, the Whitechapel bell arrived in Philadelphia and was
transported to the Pennsylvania State House. But when tested, the bell cracked,
splitting the brim. In desperate need of a communication device for the city,
Norris decided to have the bell repaired by "two ingenious workmen" who had
some experience with bell casting, John Pass and John Stow.

Pass and Stow shattered the Whitechapel bell into small fragments and melted
them in a furnace. To strengthen the casting, they added "one ounce and a half
of copper for each pound of the old bell." After two re-castings, the new bell—a
composition of about 77 percent copper and 23 percent tin—was completed.
Like its predecessor, the Pass and Stow version carried the inscription from
Leviticus.

In June 1753, the bell was placed in the State House steeple where it would
be used to call together members of the Pennsylvania Assembly for morning
and afternoon sessions, to announce the opening of the Courts of Justice, and to
gather people for a host of proclamations, including the accession of England's
King George III to the throne on February 21, 1761, and the ending of the
French-Indian War on January 26, 1763. [Nash, *Liberty Bell*, 9-12].

During the late eighteenth century, the State House Bell witnessed a host of
significant political events, leading Americans of a later era to associate it with
political liberty. [*Ibid.*, pp. 13-20].

54 Murphy, *op. cit.*, pp. 285-86.

55 L. Treese, *The Storm Gathering: The Penn Family and the American Revolution*
(University Park, PA: Penn State Press, 1992), p. 7. In 1712, Penn reduced the
asking price from 20,000 pounds to the 12,000 pounds Queen Mary of England
was willing to pay. But when he suffered a severe stroke in October of that year
the deal was suspended. His wife, Hannah, tried to revive the negotiations, but
objections from her stepson, William Jr, who viewed Pennsylvania as part of his
inheritance, and her son-in-law, William Aubrey, who viewed the colony as an
on-going source of income, eliminated that possibility. [S. Drinker, *Hannah Penn
and the Proprietorship of Pennsylvania*. (Philadelphia: National Society of the
Colonial Dames of America in Pennsylvania, 1958), pp. 32-35].

56 Murphy, *op. cit.*, pp. 352-55.

57 Treese, *op. cit.*, pp. 7-8.

58 R. Dunn. "Penny Wise and Pound Foolish: Penn as a Businessman," in Dunn
& Dunn (1986), *op. cit.*, pp. 37-54. Richard Dunn claims that Penn spent more
money than he had, failed to collect quitrents from those who settled in his
colony and hired untrustworthy financial advisers.

59 M. Dunn, "The Personality of William Penn," in Dunn & Dunn (1986), *op.
cit.*, p. 11. Mary Maples Dunn argues that Penn "maintained an emotional
distance from others including his family." She also points out that Penn "loved
a whirlwind life," that kept him away from home. Thus, he was an "absentee
father a good deal of the time."

Chapter 3

1 F. Tolles, *Meeting House & Counting House: The Quaker Merchants of
Colonial Philadelphia, 1682–1763* (Chapel Hill: University of North Carolina
Press, 1948), pp. 113-24.

2 Kashatus, *op. cit.*, pp. 42-45.

3 J. Marietta, *The Reformation of American Quakerism, 1748–1783*
(Philadelphia: University of Pennsylvania Press, 1984), pp. 103-104.

4 *Ibid.*, pp. 3-30. According to Marietta, the laxity of discipline among
   Philadelphia Quakers, both male and female members increased dramatically
   between 1720 and 1780. There were a variety of offenses, including but not
   limited to fornication, drunkenness, indebtedness, and military activity.

5 Treese, *op. cit.*, pp. 7-12, 19-22, 35-40.

6 M. Bacon, *The Quiet Rebels: The Story of Quakers in America* (New York:
   Basic Books, 1969), pp. 65-66, 69.

7 Marietta, *op. cit.*, pp. 189-91.

8 R. Wilson, *Philadelphia Quakers, 1681-1981* (Philadelphia: Philadelphia Yearly
   Meeting, 1981), p. 44.

9 Marietta, *op. cit.*, pp. 42-45.

10 Marietta, *op. cit.*, pp. 150-58.

11 R. Jones, *The Quakers in the American Colonies* (New York: Macmillan, 1911),
    p. 503.

12 Treese, op. *cit.*, pp. 55-57.

13 Treese, *op. cit.*, pp. 58-60.

14 Marietta, *op. cit.*, pp. 205-209.

15 Treese, *op. cit.*, pp. 151-56.

16 Philadelphia Yearly Meeting, *Minutes*: 9 mo. 28, 1776. Quaker Collection,
    Haverford College. Hereafter cited as PYM, *Minutes*.

17 Bacon, *op. cit.*, p. 72.

18 Jones, *op. cit.*, pp. 564-65.

19 A. Mekeel, *The Quakers and the American Revolution* (York, England: Sessions
    Book Trust, 1996), pp. 229-30. Mekeel, in an earlier 1979 edition of his book,
    failed to distinguish between those members whose cases were "dealt with" by
    Philadelphia Yearly Meeting and those who were actually "disowned" by PYM
    for violating the peace testimony. Thus, while the Yearly Meeting disowned
    948 members for various violations, the total number of offenders dealt with
    was 1,287, which would have been approximately 25 percent of the adult
    male Quaker membership. Similarly, military deviations accounted for 537
    dealings, resulting in 515 disownments, or 54 percent of the total disownments.
    For paying war taxes and fines there were 365 dealings, resulting in 165
    disownments or 17 percent of total disownments. The total for taking loyalty
    oaths and other war-related deviations amounted to 185 dealings, resulting in
    144 disownments, or 15 percent of total disownments. Other types of deviations
    from the peace testimony were assisting the armies in various ways, seventy-four
    dealings and thirty-two disownments; and involvement in privateers and armed
    vessels, twenty-four dealings and twenty-two disownments. [For estimation of
    Quaker population statistics, see *ibid.*, pp. 388-89].

20 W. Kashatus, *Conflict of Conviction: A Reappraisal of Quaker Involvement in
    the American Revolution.* (Lanham, MD: University Press of America, 1990),
    pp. 101-33. An examination of the backgrounds and writings of the Free
    Quakers reveals that they genuinely believed that their participation in the War
    for American Independence was consistent with the values of early Quakerism.
    They likened the Patriot cause to the same quest for world transformation
    sought by the early Quakers during the English Civil War. In fact, the Free
    Quakers admitted that they had "no new doctrines to teach," only to "pay
    regard to the principles of their Quaker forefathers as they apply to their
    own circumstances." Those "circumstances" led them to place the "liberty of
    conscience" over the peace testimony, which was, to them, "an ecclesiastical
    tyranny" at worst and a secondary doctrine at best.[Samuel Wetherill, Jr., "An
    Address to Those of the People Called Quakers, who have been Disowned

for Matters Religious or Civil," (1781) quoted in C. Wetherill, *History of the Religious Society of Friends Called by Some the Free Quakers in the City of Philadelphia* (Philadelphia: no publisher, 1894), pp. 47-49].

21 "Membership list of Free Quakers, 1781–1834," C. Wetherill, *op. cit.*, pp. 111-14. Samuel Wetherill, Jr., a Quaker textile manufacturer, was the founder of the Free Quakers. His factory produced fabrics made of wool, linen or cotton and he supplied a large quantity of woolen cloth to the Board of War during the Revolution. Since this activity that conflicted with the Quaker peace testimony, Philadelphia Yearly Meeting, in 1779, disowned Wetherill. Shortly after, he founded a small group of Quakers who were disowned for supporting the Revolutionary cause or for other reasons. They sought to continue to worship and meet as Friends in established meeting houses but were turned away. The group organized their own Society of Free Quakers in 1781. Wetherill served as clerk and supervised the building of a meeting house at Fifth and Arch Streets. This group grew to some 200 members at its height in the 1790s.

Although the Free Quakers disbanded as a religious body in 1834, the descendants of the founders preserve the Free Quaker mission of support and community aid through a foundation that makes contributions to local non-profit organizations. Today the Meeting House, at the corner of Fifth and Arch Streets in Philadelphia, is part of Independence National Historical Park and open to the public. For more information, see: freequakers.org/.

22 Mekeel (1996), *op. cit.*, pp. 198-215. Henry Drinker, a Quaker merchant, was one of the Virginia exiles. His wife, Elizabeth, kept a diary during the British occupation of Philadelphia in 1777–1778 and her effort to free her husband. Their story is the subject of R. Godbeer's *World of Trouble: A Philadelphia Quaker Family's Journey through the American Revolution* (New Haven, CT: Yale University Press, 2019).

23 E. Drinker, "Extracts from the Journal of Mrs. Henry Drinker, of Philadelphia, from September 25, 1777 to July 4, 1778," *Pennsylvania Magazine of History and Biography*, Vol. XIII, p. 306 (Philadelphia: Historical Society of Pennsylvania, 1889).

24 Godbeer, *op. cit.*, pp. 199-200.

25 Bacon, *op. cit.*, p. 73.

26 Tolles, *op. cit.*, p. 239; Barbour & Frost, *op. cit.*, pp. 128-31; Jones, *op. cit.*, pp. 573-80; and Marietta, *op. cit.* Marietta's work is the most comprehensive treatment of the Quakers' spiritual reformation. He argues that after 1755 Friends chose a sectarian course for themselves to preserve the integrity as a people and to purify their church. He details the changes that resulted in the withdrawal of Quakers from the mainstream of society and the revitalization of Philadelphia Yearly Meeting which made possible the Quakers' campaign against slavery; something that distinguished them as the first group to embrace the cause of abolitionism. Marietta's study is based on a wealth of quantitative data, most notably over 10,000 disciplinary cases in the records of Philadelphia Yearly Meeting.

27 Kashatus, *op. cit.*, pp. 81-90, 101-103.

28 J. Soderlund, *Quakers & Slavery: A Divided Spirit* (Princeton, NJ: Princeton University Press, 1985), pp. 32-53.

29 M. Rediker, *The Fearless Benjamin Lay: The Quaker Dwarf Who Became the First Revolutionary Abolitionist* (Boston: Beacon Press, 2017), pp. 4, 61-92.

30 *Ibid.*, pp. 1-2.

31 *Ibid.*, pp. 34-36

32 *Ibid.*, p. 64. Lay settled in Abington, in 1734, probably because his wife, Sarah, an itinerant Quaker minister, was a close friend of Susanna Morris, another

Quaker minister, who lived in the village. Sarah, for reasons unknown, died unexpectedly in 1735.

33 *Ibid.*, p. 114. The location of Lay cottage was on a small piece of property owned by Quakers John and Ann Phipps, on Old York Road not far from the Abington Friends Meeting House in present-day Jenkintown, Pennsylvania.

34 *Ibid.*, p. 115.

35 H. Lippincott, *The History of Abington Meeting, 1697–1949* (Jenkintown, PA: Abington Monthly Meeting, 1950), p. 45; and W. Kashatus, "Friends Fight for Freedom," *Pennsylvania Heritage*, Vol. XIV, No. 3, p. 7 (Harrisburg: Pennsylvania Historical and Museum Commission, Summer 1988).

36 Kashatus (1988), *op. cit.*, p. 7.

37 T. Drake, *Quakers and Slavery in America* (Gloucester, MA: Peter Smooth, 1965), pp. 51-52.

38 J. Woolman, *The Journal and Major Essays of John Woolman, 1740–1772*, edited by P. Moulton. (New York: Oxford University Press, 1971), pp. 24-25.

39 *Ibid.*, pp. 32-33.

40 *Ibid.*, pp. 198-209.

42 PYM, "An Epistle of Caution and Advice Concerning the Buying and Keeping of Slaves," *Minutes*: 1754.

43 PYM, Minutes: 9 mo. 28, 1758.

44 Marietta, *op. cit.*, pp. 116-19.

45 M. Jackson, *Let This Voice Be Heard: Anthony Benezet, Father of Atlantic Abolitionism* (Philadelphia: University of Pennsylvania Press, 2009), pp. 2-3.

46 Kashatus (1997), *op. cit.*, pp. 45-47; and T. Woody, *Early Quaker Education in Pennsylvania* (New York: Teacher's College, Columbia University, 1920), pp. 239-46.

47 W. Kashatus, "A Reappraisal of Anthony Benezet's Activities in Educational Reform, 1754–1784," *Quaker History*, Vol. 78, No. 1, pp. 24-36 (Haverford, PA: Friends Historical Association, 1989).

48 Jackson, *op. cit.*, pp. 215-21.

49 PYM, *Minutes*: 9 mo. 23-28, 1776.

50 H. Cadbury, "Negro Membership in the Society of Friends," *Journal of Negro History*, Vol. 21 No. 2, pp. 151-213 (Chicago: University of Chicago Press, April 1936); and D. McDaniel and V. Julye, *Fit for Freedom, Nor for Friendship: Quakers, African Americans and the Myth of Racial Justice* (Philadelphia: Friends General Conference, 2009), pp. 187-91.

51 Soderlund (1985), *op. cit.*, pp. 177, 187.

Chapter 4

1 R. Miller, "The Federal City, 1783–1800," in Weigley, *op. cit.*, pp. 161-78.

2 U.S. Bureau of the Census, "Statistics for Pennsylvania," *Thirteenth Federal Census of the United States* (Washington, D.C.: U.S. Department of Commerce and Labor, 1910), p. 569.

3 G. Nash, *Forging Freedom: The Formation of Philadelphia's Black Community, 1720–1840* (Cambridge, MA: Harvard University Press, 1988), pp. 135-37, 193, 247.

4 J. Marietta and G. Rowe, *Troubled Experiment: Crime and Justice in Pennsylvania, 1682–1800* (Philadelphia: University of Pennsylvania Press, 2006), pp. 235, 253-54

5 Scharf and Westcott, *op. cit.*, I, pp. 469, 491-93; and Powell, *op. cit.*, pp. ix-x. Between August 1 and December 15, 1793, the Yellow Fever epidemic depopulated Philadelphia. Chronicler Mathew Carey identified and published

the names of the 5,000 individuals who died and estimated that another 17,000 fled the city. [M. Carey, *A Short Account of the Malignant Fever Lately Prevalent in Philadelphia* (Philadelphia: no publisher, 1794), pp. 121-59].

6 Marietta, *op. cit.*, p. 277; and Barbour and Frost, op. cit., p. 164.

7 Bacon, *op. cit.*, pp. 93, 122-150.

8 G. Washington, "Letter to the Annual Meeting of Quakers, September, 1789," *The Papers of George Washington*, Presidential Series, edited by D. Twohig. (4 vols., Charlottesville: University Press of Virginia, 1993), IV, pp. 265–269. Washington's letter was in response to a September 28, 1789 address Philadelphia Yearly Meeting sent to the president assuring him of their firm loyalty and pledging to contribute freely to the support of the civil government. [See PYM, "An Address of the Religious Society Called Quakers, from Their Yearly Meeting for Pennsylvania, New Jersey, Delaware, and the Western Parts of Maryland and Virginia," Minutes: 9 mo. 28, 1789].

9 The phrase "Speaking Truth to Power" originated with Bayard Rustin, a Quaker civil rights activist and peace activist, who co-wrote the pamphlet *Speak Truth to Power: a Quaker Search for an Alternative to Violence* (Philadelphia: American Friends Service Committee, 1955), pp. iv-v. Internet Archive. archive.org/details/AFSCSpeakTruthToPower/page/n25/mode/2up, retrieved March 6, 2023.

10 James, *op. cit.*, pp. 49-50.

11 N. Johnston, *Eastern State Penitentiary: Crucible of Good Intentions* (Philadelphia: Philadelphia Museum of Art, 1994), pp. 21-26.

12 B. Rush quoted in M. Meranze, *Laboratories of Virtue: Punishment, Revolution and Authority in Philadelphia, 1760–1835* (Chapel Hill: University of North Carolina Press, 1996), pp. 43-44.

13 D. Rothman, *The Discovery of the Asylum: Social Order & Disorder in the New Republic* (Boston: Little Brown & Company, 1971), pp. 89-90.

14 Bacon, *op. cit.*, pp. 133-135; and Johnston, *op. cit.*, pp. 29-33, 48-53.

15 J. Haviland, "Explanation of a Design for a Penitentiary, July 2, 1821," quoted in Johnston, *op. cit.*, p. 35; and N. Teeters, "The Early Days of Eastern State Penitentiary at Philadelphia," *Pennsylvania History*. Vol. 16, pp. 261-302 (University Park: Penn State Press, October 1949).

16 Bacon, *op. cit.*, p. 139.

17 *Ibid.*, pp. 139-140; and James, *op. cit.*, pp. 205-12.

18 T. Scattergood, *Account of the rise and progress of the asylum, proposed to be established, near Philadelphia: for the relief of persons deprived of the use of their reason* (Philadelphia: no publisher, 1814), p. 6. Internet Archive. archive.org/details/2546073R.nlm.nih.gov/page/n13/mode/2up, retrieved March 6, 2023.

19 Bacon, *op. cit.*, pp. 140-41; Barbour and Frost, *op. cit.*, pp. 165-66; and Wilson, (1981), *op. cit.*, p. 115.

20 C. Cherry, *A Quiet Haven: Quakers, Moral Treatment, and Asylum Reform* (Teaneck, NJ: Fairleigh-Dickinson University Press, 1989).

21 Kashatus (1997), *op. cit.*, pp. 156-67.

22 N. Wainwright, "Age of Nicholas Biddle, 1825–1854," in Weigley, *op. cit.*, p. 297.

23 D. Labaree, *The Making of an American High School: The Credentials Market and the Central High School of Philadelphia, 1838–1939* (New Haven, CT: Yale University Press, 1988), pp. 10-12.

24 R. Kelsey, *Friends and the Indians, 1655–1917* (Philadelphia: Executive Committee of Friends on Indian Affairs, 1917), pp. 89-90; Bacon, *op. cit.*, 124-26; and Wilson (1981), *op. cit.*, 74-75.

25 M. Ream, "Philadelphia Friends and the Indians," in Moore, *op. cit.*, p. 207.

26 M. Bacon, *Mothers of Feminism: The Story of Quaker Women in America* (New York: Harper & Row, 1989 paperback), pp. 1-4.

27 T. Hamm, "Hicksite, Orthodox, and Evangelical Quakerism, 1805–1887," in Angell & Dandelion, *op. cit.*, pp. 28, 63-71. For the most complete understanding of the Hicksite Separation, see: R. Doherty, *The Hicksite Separation: A Sociological Analysis of Religious Schism in Early Nineteenth Century America* (New Brunswick, NJ: Rutgers University Press, 1967); H. Ingle, *Quakers in Conflict: The Hicksite Reformation* (Knoxville: University of Tennessee Press, 1986); and T. Hamm, *The Quakers in America* (New York: Columbia University Press, 1993). Doherty argues that changing social and economic patterns within the Society of Friends affected the individual Quaker's decision to join the more worldly, evangelical-oriented Orthodox or remain within the sectarian tradition of the Hicksite Friends. He uses a variety of quantitative data to support his argument, including wills, tax returns, city directories, and mortgage records. Ingle, on the other hand, examines the schism in the broader context of the changes taking place in American Protestantism during the nineteenth century. He argues that the city-dwelling Orthodox embraced evangelical doctrine and its emphasis on the Bible while the Hicksites, predominantly rural Friends, insisted on the primacy of personal religious experience. Hamm argues that despite their theological differences, both Orthodox and Hicksite Friends demonstrated a fundamental unity in their commitments to worship, the open ministry, and consensus decision-making. These commonalities would eventually enable both groups to reconcile their theological differences in the twentieth century.

29 E. Baltzell, *Puritan Boston and Quaker Philadelphia* (New York: Free Press, 1979), p. 437.

30 A. Wahl, "The Progressive Friends of Longwood," *Friends Historical Society Bulletin*, 42, No. 1, pp. 14-16 (Philadelphia: Friends Historical Society, Spring 1953); and C. Densmore, "Be Ye Therefore Perfect: Anti-Slavery and the and the Origins of the Yearly Meeting of Progressive Friends in Chester County, Pennsylvania," *Quaker History* Vol. 93, No. 2, pp. 28-31 (Haverford, PA: Friends Historical Association, Fall 2004).

31 "An Act for the Gradual Abolition of Slavery (1780) in *The Statutes at Large of Pennsylvania, 1682 to 1801*, edited by J. Mitchell and H. Flanders (17 vols., Harrisburg: Commonwealth of Pennsylvania, 1896–1915), Vol. X, pp. 67-73.

32 G. Nash and J. Soderlund, *Freedom By Degrees: Emancipation in Pennsylvania and its Aftermath* (New York: Oxford University, 1991), pp. 99-114.

33 I. Berlin, *Generations of Captivity: A History of African American Slaves* (Cambridge, MA: Harvard University Press, 2003), pp. 276-78.

34 Nash & Soderlund, *op. cit.*, p. 18; and Nash, *op. cit.*, pp. 213, 247.

35 W. Kashatus, *William Still: The Underground Railroad and the Angel at Philadelphia.* (South Bend, IN: Notre Dame University Press, 2021), pp. 34-35.

36 H. Mayer, *All on Fire: William Lloyd Garrison and the Abolition of Slavery* (New York: St. Martin's Press, 1998), p. 240.

37 Kashatus (2021), *op. cit.*, p. 35.

38 W. Kashatus, *Just Over the Line: Chester County and the Underground Railroad* (West Chester, PA: Chester County Historical Society & Penn State Press, 2002), pp. 63-64.

39 T. Whitson quoted in *Pennsylvania Freeman*: November 4, 1853.

40 Letter, Lucretia Mott to Martha Coffin Wright, December 5, 1861 quoted in *Selected Letters of Lucretia Coffin Mott, edited by B. Palmer, H. Ochoa and C. Faulkner (Urbana: University of Illinois Press, 2002), p. 192.*

41 Kashatus (2002), *op. cit.*, p. 64.

42 According to Thomas Garrett's biographer, James A. McGowan, the Quaker stationmaster made the claim of assisting 2,700 runaways in an April 1865 letter to William Lloyd Garrison, the editor of the anti-slavery newspaper *The Liberator*. But McGowan is skeptical of those numbers. McGowan identifies a November 1863 letter to Samuel May, an agent for the Massachusetts Anti-Slavery Society, as the last time he calculated the total numbers of fugitives he assisted, which was 2,322. In order to have assisted an additional 378 runaways by April 1865, Garrett would have had to help 126 runaways per year, or twenty-two each month. McGowan contends that this would have been nearly impossible since the traffic on Underground Railroad nearly ceased after Lincoln issued the Emancipation Proclamation in January 1863. [J. McGowan, *Station Master in the Underground Railroad: The Life and Letters of Thomas Garrett* (Jefferson, NC: McFarland & Company, 2005), pp. 115-28].

43 W. Still, *The Underground Railroad* (Philadelphia: Porter & Coates, 1872). For the database of Still's runaways as well as a multivariate analysis of the data, see: Kashatus (2021), *op. cit.*, pp. 221-277.

44 A. Cannon, *The Case of Passmore Williamson* (Philadelphia: Uriah Hunt & Son, 1856; N. Brandt and Y. Brandt, *In the Shadow of the Civil War: Passmore Williamson and the Rescue of Jane Johnson* (Columbia: University of South Carolina Press, 2007), pp. 15-16, 34-39, 81, 110-17; and Still, *op. cit.*, pp. 82-83.

45 Brandt and Brandt, *op. cit.*, pp. 83, 128-29, 136-42.

46 *Ibid.*, pp. 117, 122, 125.

47 *Ibid.*, pp. 85, 96-101, 132,

48 L. Mott quoted in Palmer, *et. al.*, *op. cit.*, p. 205.

49 Brandt and Brandt, *op. cit.*, pp. 107-10, 142, 144-51. The daring escape of Jane Johnson inspired L. Cary's compelling novel, *The Price of a Child* (New York: Random House, 1995).

50 M. Bacon, *Valiant Friend: The Life of Lucretia Mott* (New York: Walker, 1980), pp. 59-61.

51 *Ibid.*, pp. 27-35.

52 *Ibid.*, pp. 75-79.

53 *Ibid.*, pp. 86-100.

54 C. Faulkner, *Lucretia Mott's Heresy: Abolition and Women's Rights in Nineteenth-Century America* (Philadelphia: University of Pennsylvania Press, 2011), pp. 138-141.

55 E. Stanton, "Declaration of Sentiments," *Report of the Women's Right Convention Held at Seneca Falls, NY, July 19th and 20th 1848.* (Rochester, NY: no publisher, 1848). Online text, Library of Congress, www.loc.gov/item/rbcmiller001106/, retrieved March 9, 2023.

56 Faulkner, *op. cit.*, pp. 149-60.

57 *Proceedings of the Women's Rights Convention Held at West Chester, PA, June 2d and 3d, 1852* (Philadelphia: Merrihew and Thompson, 1852), 3, 6-7. Online text at Power Library digitalarchives.powerlibrary.org/papd/islandora/object/papd%3A160703, retrieved March 9, 2023.

58 Bacon (1989), *op. cit.*, pp. 126-27.

59 Faulkner, *op. cit.*, pp. 212, 215-16.

60 Quaker leadership has always been most evident in social reform. Unfortunately, there are those scholars who do not recognize Quakers as leaders because of the collective nature of their efforts, which challenges the traditional American model of leadership as "individual." [Baltzell, *op. cit.*, pp. x, 19].

Chapter 5

 1 E. Gurney, *Memoir and Correspondence of Eliza P. Gurney*, edited by R.
    Mott. (Philadelphia: J.B. Lippincott, 1884), pp. 309-313. The original memoir
    of Lincoln's interview with the Quaker delegation is in the collections of the
    Historical Society of Pennsylvania.
 2 Letter, Abraham Lincoln to Eliza P. Gurney, Washington, D.C., October 26,
    1862, quoted in *The Collected Works of Abraham Lincoln*, edited by R. Basler.
    (8 vols. New Brunswick, NJ: Rutgers University Press, 1953–1955),
    V, p. 478.
 3 W. Kashatus, *Abraham Lincoln, the Quakers, and the Civil War* (Santa Barbara,
    CA: Praeger, 2014), pp. 5-6.
 4 For Lincoln's reference to his Quaker ancestry, see *The Chester County Times*
    (West Chester, PA): February 11, 1860. For Lincoln's Quaker genealogy, see D.
    Keiser, "Quaker Ancestors of Lincoln," *Lincoln Herald*, Vol. 63, pp. 134-137
    (Harrogate, TN: Abraham Lincoln Library & Museum, 1961); and H. Cadbury,
    "The Hunt for Lincoln's Quaker Ancestors," *Friends Journal* Vol. 12, No. 3,
    pp. 57-58 (Philadelphia: Religious Society of Friends, February 1, 1966). Keiser
    and Cadbury identify Mordecai Lincoln, the great-great-grandfather of the
    president, as having settled in Exeter Township, Berks County, Pennsylvania, in
    1733. Mordecai's sons, Abraham and John, married into the Quaker religion.
    Abraham (born 1736) married Ann Boone, a Quaker, in 1760. John (born in
    1716) married Rebecca Flower, a third-generation Quaker.
 5 Lincoln's "Quaker" traits are identified in J. Suppinger, "The Intimate Lincoln,"
    Lincoln Herald, Vol. 85, No. 3, p. 161 (Harrogate, TN: Abraham Lincoln
    Library and Museum, Fall 1983).
 6 A. Guelzo, *Abraham Lincoln: Redeemer President* (Grand Rapids, MI: William
    B. Eerdmans Publishing Company, 1999), p. 151.
 7 Letter, Lincoln to Gurney, October 26, 1862 in Basler, *op. cit.*, p. 478.
 8 Kashatus (2014), *op. cit.*, p. 26.
 9 *Ibid.*, p. 26.
10 Garrison quoted in McDaniel and Julye, *op. cit.*, p. 146.
11 Kashatus (2014), *op. cit.*, p. 89.
12 Palmer, quoted in J. Weber, "'If Ever War Was Holy': Quaker Soldiers and the
    Union Army," *North and South*, Vol. 5, No. 5, p. 66 (Tollhouse, CA: The Civil
    War Society, April 2002).
13 Kashatus (2014), *op. cit.*, p. 99.
14 *Ibid.*, p. 76.
15 *Ibid.*, p. 100.
16 United States Congress, "Amendment to the Enrollment Act of 1863,"
    (February 15, 1864) quoted in R. Russell, "Development of Conscientious
    Objector Recognition in the United States," *George Washington Law Review*
    (Washington, D.C.), Vol. 20, No. 4, pp. 418-420 (Washington, D.C.: George
    Washington University, March 1952).
17 Kashatus (2014), *op. cit.*, pp. 100-101.
18 Letter, Eliza Gurney to Abraham Lincoln, Earlham Lodge: September 8, 1864 in
    R. Mott, *op. cit.*, p. 321.
19 J. McPherson, *Ordeal By Fire: The Civil War and Reconstruction* (New York:
    McGraw-Hill, 2001), pp. 385-86.
20 Kashatus (2014), *op. cit.*, p. 77.
21 *Ibid.*, 98.

22 Chaplain of the 14th Wisconsin Volunteers quoted in A. Sharp, "Victims of Two Enemies: The Quakers in the Civil War," *Evangelical Friend* Vol. 11, No. 3, p. 7 (Alliance, OH: Evangelical Friends Alliance, November 1978).

23 Kashatus (2014), *op. cit.*, pp. 104-105.

24 Lucretia Mott quoted in P. Benjamin, *The Philadelphia Quakers in the Industrial Age, 1865–1920* (Philadelphia: Temple University Press, 1976), p. 130.

25 Kashatus (2014), *op. cit.*, p. 105.

26 *Ibid.*, pp. 105-107.

27 *Ibid.*, p 122. During its years of operation, the Freedmen's Bureau fed millions of former slaves, built hospitals and provided medical aid, negotiated labor contracts, and settled labor disputes. It also assisted black military veterans, helped ex-slaves legalize marriages, and locate lost relatives. The bureau also was instrumental in building thousands of schools for blacks, and helped to found such colleges as Howard University in Washington, D.C., Fisk University in Nashville, Tennessee, and Hampton University in Hampton, Virginia.

Despite these successes, the Freedmen's Bureau was short-lived because it lacked a clear mandate in regard to its proper authority and relied on private charity and annual congressional appropriations for its survival. Organized by the War Department, the bureau was made subject to presidential authority by a Radical Republican Congress that made it increasingly responsible for the success of congressional Reconstruction. After the war, the bureau's mission and authority were compromised by opposition in the South and inconsistent support in Washington. Finally, in the summer of 1872, Congress, responding in part to pressure from white Southerners, dismantled the Freedmen's Bureau. [P. *Cimbala and R. Miller, editors, The Freedmen's Bureau and Reconstruction* (New York: Fordham University Press,1999), pp. xvi-xxx].

28 Kashatus (2014), *op. cit.*, p. 107.

29 Whittier quoted in *Life and Letters of John Greenleaf Whittier*, edited by S. Pickard. (2 vols., London: Sampson, Lowe, Marston & Co., 1895), II, pp. 486-87. Fearing they might lose the 1864 elections, Radical Republicans nominated Tennessee Democrat Andrew Johnson as vice-president replacing Hannibal Hamlin of Maine to court a broader constituency. They also enlisted military heroes to campaign for the Lincoln ticket and conducted mass rallies to build support for the party. [R. Engs and R. Miller, *The Birth of the Grand Old* Party: *The Republicans' First Generation* (Philadelphia: University of Pennsylvania Press, 2002), pp. 10-11].

30 Kashatus (2014), *op. cit.*, pp. 111-13.

31 Letter, Gurney to Lincoln, September 8, 1864 in Mott, *op. cit.*, p. 321.

32 Member of Sanitary Commission and Lincoln quoted in E. Hertz, *Lincoln Talks* (New York: Viking, 1939), p. 580.

33 J. McPherson, *Battle Cry of Freedom: The Civil War Era* (New York: Oxford University Press, 1988), p. 805.

34 Kashatus (2014), *op. cit.*, p. 113. The Emancipation Proclamation transformed the ideology of the Republican Party as well as the objective of the Civil War. At the outbreak of the war, Lincoln's sole aim was to preserve the Union. He realized that he would not be able to retain the loyalty of the border slave states if he abolished slavery. But as the war unfolded many northerners, especially abolitionists and Radical Republicans in Congress, insisted that slavery must become a military target to achieve victory. As slaves abandoned southern plantations and the manpower needs of the Union Army increased, danger of losing the border states receded and Lincoln felt more confident to free the slaves.

While his executive order did not liberate all the slaves—only those under Confederate control—it did make emancipation a war aim every bit as important as preserving the Union. It also transformed the ideology of the Republican Party into one that embraced not only the defeat of slavery but also equal protection under the law regardless of race. [E. Foner, "The Ideology of the Republican Party," in Engs and Miller, *op. cit.*, pp. 10-11].

35 Kashatus (2014), *op. cit.*, p. 114.

Chapter 6

1 N. Burt and W. Davies, "The Iron Age, 1876–1905," in Weigley, *op. cit.*, pp. 477-83; and P. Scranton, *Proprietary Capitalism: The Textile Manufacture at Philadelphia, 1800–1885* (Cambridge, England: Cambridge University Press, 2003), pp. 42-48, 314-352.

2 D. Beers, "The Centennial City, 1865–1876," Weigley, *op. cit.*, p. 469.

3 E. Wolf, *Philadelphia: Portrait of an American City* (Philadelphia: Camino Press & The Library Company of Philadelphia, 1990), p. 244.

4 G. Harrison, *The Remains of William Penn. Pennsylvania's Plea, The Mission to England, Visit to the Grave. Letters, Etc.* (Philadelphia: Globe Printing House, 1882), pp. 9-11, 81-84.

5 Letter, editor of the *London Times*, from G. Harrison, London, July 22, 1881 quoted in *ibid.*, pp. 47-52. Harrison summarized his meeting with Penn's heirs in this letter to the editor.

6 Letter, D. Parrish to Honorable John Welsh, Dresden, England, May 23, 1881; and letter, D. Parrish to George Harrison, Dresden, England, July 6, 1881 in *ibid.*, pp. 84-85.

7 Letter, Peter Penn Gaskell to Jonathan Littleboy, London, July 6, 1881; and letter, Jonathan Littleboy to George Harrison, Watford, England, July 19, 1881 quoted in *ibid.*, pp. 90-92.

8 W. Kashatus, "Images of William Penn: An Evolving Portrait of Pennsylvania's Founding Father," in *An Image of Peace: The Penn Treaty Collection of Mr. and Mrs. Meyer P. Potamkin* (Harrisburg, PA: Pennsylvania Museum and Historical Commission, 1996), p. 13; and Burt and Davies, "Iron Age, 1876–1905," in Weigley, *op. cit.*, pp. 506-508.

9 G. Gurney, "Alexander Milne Calder: William Penn," *in Fairmount Park Art Association, Sculpture of a City: Philadelphia's Treasures in Bronze and Stone* (New York: Walker, 1974), pp. 104-109.

10 Joshua Baily quoted in P. Benjamin, *op. cit.*, p. 51.

11 Benjamin, *op. cit.*, pp. 54-55, 79.

12 *Ibid.*, pp. 49, 55-56.

13 *Ibid.*, pp. 57-58, 88.

14 "Joseph Wharton is Dead. Prominent Ironmaker Expires at Home in Philadelphia," *New York Times,* January 12, 1909.

15 K. Fitzgerald and E. Reinhardt, "The Legacy and Philanthropy of Anna Thomas Jeanes," *Friends Journal Online* (March 1, 2020) www.friendsjournal.org/the-legacy-and-philanthropy-of-anna-thomas-jeanes/, retrieved March 10, 2023.

16 *Ibid.*

17 For information on the various bequests made by Anna T. Jeanes, see: Swarthmore College, *Papers on the Bequest of the late Anna T. Jeanes* (Legare Street Press, 2022).

18 Wilson (1981), *op. cit.*, p. 109; and Benjamin, *op. cit.*, pp. 146-147.

19 Fitzgerald and Reinhardt, *op. cit.*

20 Benjamin, *op. cit.*, pp. 85-87.

21 *Ibid.*, pp. 69-72.

22. R. Miller and T. Marzik, *Immigrants and Religion in Urban America* (Philadelphia: Temple University Press, 1977), pp. xiv-xv.

23 C. Milner, *With Good Intentions: Quaker Work among the Pawnees, Otos, and Omahas in 1870s* (Lincoln: University of Nebraska Press, 1982), pp. 1-26.

24 *Ibid.*, *op. cit.*, pp. 24, 119-20.

25 Benjamin, *op. cit.*, pp. 112-14.

26 R. Kelsey, *op. cit.*, pp. 189-191.

27 Benjamin, *op. cit.*, pp. 113-15.

28 Milner, *op. cit.*, pp. 187-99.

29 Wolf, *op. cit.*, pp. 237-38.

30 Matthew S. Quay quoted in Lincoln Steffens, "Philadelphia: Corrupt and Contented," *McLure's Magazine,* Vol. 21, No. 3, pp. 249-250 (New York: S.S. McClure, July 1903).

31 T. Speakman, "How Far Should Friends Take Part in Public Affairs?" *Friends Intelligencer*, Vol. XLIV, pp. 65-66 (Philadelphia: Religious Society of Friends, January 28, 1887).

32 Benjamin, *op. cit.*, p. 75.

33 Benjamin, *op. cit.*, pp. 77-78.

34 Burt and Davies, *op. cit.*, p. 498.

35 J. Burkhart and R. West, " *... better than riches": A Tricentennial History of William Penn Charter School* (Philadelphia: William Penn Charter School, 1989), pp. 37-40.

36 E. Bronner, "A Time of Change: Philadelphia Yearly Meeting, 1861–1914," in Moore, *op. cit.*, p. 107.

37 Wilson (1981), *op. cit.*, pp. 94-95.

38 Benjamin, *op. cit.*, p. 35.

39 Wilson (1981), *op. cit.*, pp. 98-99.

40 Baltzell, *op. cit.*, pp. 444-46.

Chapter 7

1 Bacon (1969), *op. cit.*, p. 182.

2 Barbour and Frost, *op. cit.*, p. 251.

3 R. Jones, *A Service of Love in Wartime: American Friends Relief Work in Europe, 1917–1919* (New York: Macmillan, 1920), pp. 7-9; and J. Frost, "'Our Deeds Carry Our Message': The Early History of the American Friends Service Committee," *Quaker History*, Vol. 81, No. 1, pp. 1-50 (Haverford, PA: Friends Historical Association, Spring 1992).

4 Jones (1920), *op. cit.*, p. 9.

5 *Ibid.*, pp. 17-22.

6 Mary Hoxie Jones, *Swords into Ploughshares: An Account of the American Friends Service Committee, 1917–1937* (New York: Macmillan, 1937), pp. 18-20.

7 *Ibid.*, pp. 42-50; and Bacon (1969), *op. cit.*, p. 183.

8 M. Bacon, *Let This Life Speak: The Legacy of Henry Joel Cadbury* (Philadelphia: University of Pennsylvania Press, 1987), pp. 37-48.

9 Jones (1920), *op. cit.*, pp. 227-43.

10 Bacon (1969), *op. cit.*, p. 184.

11 *Ibid.*, pp. 184-85.

12　*Ibid.*, pp. 186-87.

13　H. Cadbury, "Urges Good Will by Jews for Nazis; Prof. Cadbury of Society of Friends Says It Will Gain More Than Will Hate," *New York Times*, June 15, 1934.

14　"Nazis Smash, Loot, Burn Jewish Shops and Temples until Goebbels Calls Halt," *New York Times*, November 11, 1938.

15　R. Jones, "Our Day in the German Gestapo," *The American Friend*, Vol. 35, No. 14, p. 265 (Philadelphia: Religious Society of Friends, July 10, 1947).

16　L. Miller, *Witness for Humanity: A Biography of Clarence E. Picket* (Wallingford, PA: Pendle Hill Press, 1999), pp. 195-214.

17　H. Cadbury quoted in "Acceptance Speech for the American Friends Service Committee on the occasion of the award of the Nobel Peace Prize in Oslo, December 10, 1947," NobelPrize.org, www.nobelprize.org/prizes/peace/1947/friends-committee/acceptance-speech/, retrieved March 14, 2023.

18　T. Hamm, *The Quakers in America* (New York: Columbia University Press, 2003), pp. 54-56.

19　H. Hadley, "Diminishing Separation: Philadelphia Yearly Meetings Reunite, 1915–1955," in Moore, *op. cit.*, pp. 151-68; and Hamm (2002), *op. cit.*, pp. 60-63.

20　Hadley, *op. cit.*, pp. 168-72.

21　M. Jones, "Philadelphia Yearly Meeting and the American Friends Service Committee," in Moore, *op. cit.*, p. 240; and Barbour and Frost, *op. cit.*, pp. 254-57.

22　 B. Rustin, *op. cit.*

23　McDaniel and Julye, *op. cit.*, pp. 270-72.

24　*Ibid.*, pp. 273-75.

25　*W. Colon, T. Heriza, and T. Histand, "Love in Action: A Brief History of AFSC's Work in the Past 100 Years," (May 18, 2017) AFSC.org,* afsc.org/news/love-action-brief-history-afscs-work-past-100-years, *retrieved March 14, 2023.*

Chapter 8

1　Philadelphia Yearly Meeting, "2020 Membership Statistics," *State of Philadelphia Meeting Reports, 2020,* www.pym.org/sessions/wp-content/uploads/sites/7/2021/07/Membership-Statistics-2020-PDF-20210727.pdf, retrieved March 14, 2023. Statistics completed based on information received as of July 11, 2021. The membership of Philadelphia Yearly Meeting was about 30,000 members in 1775. By 1925, the number of members dropped to 15,000 and they were unevenly divided between the two yearly meetings. The 1955 reunification brought together 5,537 Orthodox and 11,633 Hicksites Friends, for a total membership of about 17,000. By 1994, Philadelphia Yearly Meeting had just 12,100 members. Since then, the membership has dropped to just over 10,000 Friends.

　　Today there are about 75,000 Quakers in the United States, but they belong two three distinct organizations: (1) Friends General Conference, which is comprised of Quakers primarily on the East Coast, observes unprogrammed worship and has the most liberal tradition of all American Quakers; (2) Friends United Meeting, which is comprised of Quakers who live mostly in the Mid-West and observe programmed worship in the pastoral tradition; and (3) Evangelical Friends Alliance, which is located on the West Coast and is the most Christ-centered of the three traditions.

　　Worldwide, there are more than 300,000 Quakers who embrace one of the three above-mentioned traditions. The highest percentage of these Quakers are in Africa and were the result of a missionary effort by Evangelical Friends in the early twentieth century.

2 D. McCormick, "Can Quakerism Survive?" *Friends Journal* Vol. 16, pp. 15-17 (Philadelphia: Religious Society of Friends, February 2018). McCormick points out that there are relatively few young members and attenders and many (if not most) of our meetings are primarily made up of aging baby boomers. He fears that the greying of the Society of Friends will eventually result in the death of Quakerism in the United States because there will not be any younger members to replace them.

3 Michael Sheeran offers a compelling example of servant leadership among Friends in his examination of the role of the clerk in the decision-making process of a business meeting. [M. Sheeran, *Beyond Majority Rule: Voteless Decisions in the Religious Society of Friends* (Philadelphia: Philadelphia Yearly Meeting, 1996), pp. 91-108]. Larry Spears offers a more general description of Quaker Servant Leadership. [L. Spears, "Servant-Leadership and Quakers," *Quaker Life* Volume 2, No. 3, pp. 5-7 (Richmond, IN: Friends United Press, July–August 2003).

4 Quaker historian and author Howard H. Brinton shows that the religious philosophies of Quakerism's founders—George Fox, Robert Barclay, and William Penn—were firmly rooted in the New Testament Gospel of John and that the Society of Friends was founded as a Christian movement. [See: Brinton, *The Religious Philosophy of Quakerism: The Beliefs of Fox, Barclay and Penn as based on the Gospel of John* (Wallingford, PA: Pendle Hill Publications, 1973)].

5 In June 1979, a cover article in *The New Republic* attacked the AFSC for abandoning the Quakers' traditional witness to peace. [S. Chapman, "Shot From Guns: The Lost Pacifism of American Quakers," *The New Republic* Vol. 180, No. 21, pp. 27-36 (June 9, 1979). Another expression of concern appeared in 1987 by Guenter Lewy, a German Jew and early member of the 1960s peace movement. In his book, *Peace & Revolution: The Moral Crisis of American Pacifism* (William B. Eerdmans, 1987), Lewy repeated the charges that AFSC had abandoned their historic peace testimony as well as their church. But he went even further than Chapman.

Lewy argued that AFSC's active role in providing relief supplies and medical aid to the North Vietnamese and the Viet Cong during the Vietnam conflict did not produce peace, but furthered evils, including the exodus of boat people and the Khmer Rouge genocide in Cambodia. In the process, AFSC abandoned a longstanding, but informal, prohibition on assisting Marxist groups. For Lewy, AFSCs involvement with the North Vietnamese and the Viet Cong represented the "victory of radical leftist tendencies within the organization" and its "alignment with violent and totalitarian forces in that country and later in Central America." Lewy's argument was difficult to deny because he defended his assertions with extensive research from the AFSC archives. But that did not prevent Quaker activist and author Chuck Fager from challenging Lewy's interpretation.

In 1988, Fager edited and published his own book of essays by more than a dozen authors, including John Sullivan, James Matlack, and Elise Boulding. Collectively their essays attack Lewy's research, intentions, and outlook, and defend AFSC against his criticisms. Fager was objective enough to give the proverbial "last word" to Lewy, who contributed a concluding response. [C. Fager, editor, *Quaker Service at the Crossroads,* (Bellefonte, PA: Kimo Press, 1988).

Interestingly, Fager, two decades later, appeared to become just as disillusioned by AFSC as Chapman and Lewy, but for a different reason—the apathy among those Quakers who still belonged to the organization. "AFSC

has essentially dropped off the radar screen for active American Friends," Fager
wrote in 2010. "Activists aren't against it; we've just quit thinking about it.
It's mainly 'divorced' from our life as a faith community. It's become one more
group with an agenda and fund appeals, one more envelope in the pile." [See:
Fager, "AFSC & Quakers: The Background of a Concern," *A Friendly Letter*,
June 19, 2010, afriendlyletter.com/afsc-quakers-i-the-background-of-a-concern/,
retrieved March 9, 2023].

6 For information on the growth and accomplishments of Catholic activism, see:
U.S. Conference of Catholic Bishops, "A Pastoral Letter on War and Peace,"
(Washington, D.C.: U.S. Conference of Catholic Bishops, 1983); S. Keogh and
R. Wood, "The Rebirth of Catholic Collective Action in Central America: A new
model of church-based political participation," *Social Compass* Vol. 60, No. 2
(2013): pp. 273–291; T. Cordaro, "The Catholic Peace Movement: dying and
rising," *National Catholic Reporter*: October 5, 2013; E. Schlosser, "Break-In
At Y-12: How a handful of pacifists and nuns exposed the vulnerability of
America's nuclear-weapons sites," *The New Yorker* (March 9, 2015): pp. 46-69;
K. Oakes, "Meet the pioneers who made way for Catholic activists today. The
legacy of towering figures such as Dorothy Day and Daniel Berigan still guides
the work of Catholic activists today," *U.S. Catholic*. Vol. 84, No. 2 (February
2019): pp. 12-16; Oakes, "What is social action in the church today? A new
generation of Catholic activists is finding its voice," *U.S. Catholic*. Vol. 84,
No. 3 (March 2019), pp. 9-12; and M. Walther, "This is Why America Needs
Catholicism," *The New York Times*: July 30, 2021.

7 For information on the thirty-eight Quaker schools in the Philadelphia area, see:
Friends Council on Education online at www.friendscouncil.org/.

8 Information on the tuitions and Quaker enrollments for the thirty-eight Quaker
schools in the Philadelphia area was accessed online from each on the school's
websites. The tuitions listed were for the 2023–2024 academic year. Note that
most of the schools offer need-based financial aid and there is scholarship
assistance for the children of Quaker families available from Philadelphia
Yearly meeting and the Friends Council on education. But the scholarships only
amount to $2,000 at most.

9 C. Flanagan, "Private Schools Have Become Truly Obscene," *The Atlantic*:
April 2021, www.theatlantic.com/magazine/archive/2021/04/private-schools-
are-indefensible/618078/, retrieved March 15, 2023; F. Lascroux, "The Toxic
Influence of the Private School System," *Education International*: December
14, 2022, www.ei-ie.org/en/item/27172:the-toxic-influence-of-the-private-
school-system, retrieved March 15, 2023; and J. Holland, "'Snowplow Parents'
and the Pressure at Top Private Schools," *Washingtonian*: October 9, 2011,
www.washingtonian.com/2011/10/09/snowplow-parents-and-the-pressure-at-
top-private-schools/, retrieved March 15, 2023.

10 Tolles, *op. cit.*

11 D. Hogan, "The Market Revolution and Disciplinary Power: Joseph Lancaster
and the Psychology of the Early Classroom System," *History of Education
Quarterly*. Vol. 29, No. 3, pp. 381-417 (Cambridge, UK: Cambridge University
Press, Fall 1989).

12 Burkhart and West, *op. cit.*, pp. 37-40.

Bibliography

Primary Sources

Cadbury, H., "Acceptance Speech for the American Friends Service Committee on the occasion of the award of the Nobel Peace Prize in Oslo, December 10, 1947." NobelPrize.org. Cadbury, H., "Urges Good Will by Jews for Nazis; Prof. Cadbury of Society of Friends Says It Will Gain More Than Will Hate," *New York Times*, June 15, 1934.

Cannon, A., *The Case of Passmore Williamson* (Philadelphia: Uriah Hunt & Son, 1856).

Carey, M., *A Short Account of the Malignant Fever Lately Prevalent in Philadelphia* (Philadelphia: no publisher, 1794).

Drinker, E., "Extracts from the Journal of Mrs. Henry Drinker, of Philadelphia, from September 25, 1777 to July 4, 1778," *Pennsylvania Magazine of History and Biography,* Vol. XIII, pp. 208-308 (Philadelphia: Historical Society of Pennsylvania, 1889).

Fox, G., *Cain against Abel, Representing New England's Church Hierarchy in Opposition to Her Christian Protestant Dissenters* (London: no publisher, 1675).

Fox, G., *Journal of George Fox,* edited by J. Nickalls. (Philadelphia: Religious Society of Friends, 1985).

Gaskell, P. to J. Littleboy, London, July 6, 1881 in G. Harrison, *The Remains of William Penn. Pennsylvania's Plea, The Mission to England, Visit to the Grave. Letters, Etc.* (Philadelphia: Globe Printing House, 1882), 90-91.

Gurney, E., to A. Lincoln, Earlham Lodge: September 8, 1864 in *Memoir and Correspondence of Eliza P. Gurney*, edited by R. Mott. (Philadelphia: J.B. Lippincott, 1884), pp. 321-322.

Harrison, G. to editor of *London Times*, London, July 22, 1881 in G. Harrison, *The Remains of William Penn. Pennsylvania's Plea, The Mission to England, Visit to the Grave. Letters, Etc.* (Philadelphia: Globe Printing House, 1882), pp. 47-52.

Harrison, G., *The Remains of William Penn. Pennsylvania's Plea, The Mission to England, Visit to the Grave. Letters, Etc.* (Philadelphia: Globe Printing House, 1882).

Haviland, J., "Explanation of a Design for a Penitentiary, July 2, 1821," quoted in N. Johnston, *Eastern State Penitentiary: Crucible of Good Intentions* (Philadelphia: Philadelphia Museum of Art, 1994), p. 35.

Jones, R., *A Service of Love in Wartime: American Friends Relief Work in Europe, 1917–1919* (New York: Macmillan, 1920).

Jones, R., "Our Day in the German Gestapo," *The American Friend*, Vol. 35, No. 14, p. 265 (Philadelphia: Religious Society of Friends, July 10, 1947).

"Joseph Wharton is Dead. Prominent Ironmaker Expires at Home in Philadelphia," *New York Times,* January 12, 1909.

Lincoln, A., to E. Gurney, Washington, D.C., October 26, 1862 in *The Collected Works of Abraham Lincoln*, edited by R.P. Basler. 8 vols. (New Brunswick, NJ: Rutgers University Press, 1953–1955), V, p. 478.

Littleboy, J. to G. Harrison, Watford, England, July 19, 1881 in G. Harrison, *The Remains of William Penn. Pennsylvania's Plea, The Mission to England, Visit to the Grave. Letters, Etc.* (Philadelphia: Globe Printing House, 1882),   pp. 91-92.

Mott, L., *Selected Letters of Lucretia Coffin Mott, edited by B. W. Palmer, H. B. Ochoa, and C. Faulkner.* (Urbana: University of Illinois Press, 2002).

Parrish, D. to G. Harrison, Dresden, England, July 6,1881 in G. Harrison, *The Remains of William Penn. Pennsylvania's Plea, The Mission to England, Visit to the Grave. Letters, Etc.* (Philadelphia: Globe Printing House, 1882), pp. 84-85.

Parrish, D. to J. Welsh, Dresden, England, May 23, 1881 in G. Harrison, *The Remains of William Penn. Pennsylvania's Plea, The Mission to England, Visit to the Grave. Letters, Etc.* (Philadelphia: Globe Printing House, 1882), p. 84.

Pastorius, F., "Germantown Protest Against Slavery," (1688) in *Pennsylvania History: Essays and Documents*, edited by J. Davis and P. Newman (New York: Prentice Hall, 2010), pp. 56-57.

Penn, W., *A Collection of the Works of William Penn*, edited by J. Besse (2 vols. London, 1726).

Penn, W., "An Account of the Convincement of William Penn Delivered by Himself to Thomas Harvey," (1677) *Journal of Friends Historical Society*, Vol. 32, pp. 22-26 (Philadelphia: Friends Historical Society, 1935).

Penn, W., "A Further Account of the Province of Pennsylvania," (1685) edited by A. Myers, *Narratives of Early Pennsylvania, West New Jersey and Delaware, 1630–1707* (New York: Charles Scribner's Sons, 1912), pp. 255-267.

Penn, W., "A Short Advertisement upon the Situation and Extent of the City of Philadelphia and the ensuing Platform thereof, by the Surveyor-General," (1683) *The Papers of William Penn, 1660–1726,* edited by R. Dunn and M. Dunn (5 vols., Philadelphia: University of Pennsylvania Press, 1981–1986), II, pp. 458-60.

Penn, W., "Last Will and Testament, October 30, 1701," in *The Papers of William Penn, 1660–1726,* edited by R. Dunn and M. Dunn. (5 vols., Philadelphia: University of Pennsylvania Press, 1981–1986), IV, pp. 112-15.

Penn, W., *The Papers of William Penn, 1660–1726,* edited by R. Dunn and M. Dunn (5 vols., Philadelphia: University of Pennsylvania Press, 1981–1986).

Penn, W., *William Penn and the founding of Pennsylvania, 1680–1684: A Documentary History*, edited by J. Soderlund. (Philadelphia: University of Pennsylvania Press, 1983).

Penn, W., *William Penn's Own Account of the Lenni Lenape or Delaware Indians* (1683), edited by A. Myers. (Wallingford, PA: Middle Atlantic Press, 1970).

Pennsylvania Assembly, "An Act for the Gradual Abolition of Slavery (1780) in *The Statutes at Large of Pennsylvania, 1682 to 1801*, edited by J. Mitchell and H. Flanders. Vol. X, pp. 67-73 (17 vols., Harrisburg, PA: Commonwealth of Pennsylvania, 1896–1915).

Pepys, S., *Diary, 1661–1689,* online edition at www.pepysdiary.com.

Philadelphia Yearly Meeting, *Minutes, 1754–1820* Microfilm copy. Quaker Collection, Haverford College, Haverford, Pennsylvania.

Philadelphia Yearly Meeting (Hicksite), *Minutes, 1827–1955* Microfilm copy. Friends Historical Library, Swarthmore College, Swarthmore, Pennsylvania.

Philadelphia Yearly Meeting (Orthodox), *Minutes, 1827–1955* Microfilm copy. Quaker Collection, Haverford College, Haverford, Pennsylvania.

Proceedings of the Women's Rights Convention Held at West Chester, PA, June 2d and 3d, 1852. (Philadelphia: Merrihew and Thompson, 1852).

Rustin, B., *Speak Truth to Power: A Quaker Search for an Alternative to Violence* (Philadelphia: American Friends Service Committee, 1955).

Scattergood, T., *Account of the rise and progress of the asylum, proposed to be established, near Philadelphia; for the relief of persons deprived of the use of their reason* (Philadelphia: no publisher, 1814).

Speakman, T., "How Far Should Friends Take Part in Public Affairs?" *Friends Intelligencer*, Vol. XLIV, pp. 65-66 (Philadelphia: Religious Society of Friends, January 28, 1887).

Stanton, E., "Declaration of Sentiments," *Report of the Women's Rights Convention Held at Seneca Falls, NY, July 19th and 20th 1848.* Rochester, NY, 1848, online text, Library of Congress, www.loc.gov/item/rbcmiller001106/.

Steffens, L. "Philadelphia: Corrupt and Contented," *McLure's Magazine,* Vol. 21, No. 3, pp. 249-263 (New York: S.S. McClure, July 1903).

Still, W., *The Underground Railroad* (Philadelphia: Porter & Coates, 1872).

United States Congress, "Amendment to the Enrollment Act of 1863," (February 15, 1864) quoted in R. Russell, "Development of Conscientious Objector Recognition in the United States," *George Washington Law Review* (Washington, D.C.), Vol. 20, No. 4, pp. 418-420 (Washington, D.C.: George Washington University, March 1952):

Washington, G., *Papers of George Washington*, Presidential Series, edited by D. Twohig (4 vols., Charlottesville: University Press of Virginia, 1993).

Whittier, J., *Life and Letters of John Greenleaf Whittier*, edited by S. Pickard (2 vols., London: Sampson, Lowe, Marston & Co., 1895).

Woolman, J., *Journal and Major Essays of John Woolman*, edited by P. Moulton (New York: Oxford University Press, 1971).

Secondary Sources

Allen, R. "Restoration Quakerism, 1660–1691," in S. Angel, S., and P. Dandelion, editors, *Oxford Handbook of Quaker Studies* (New York: Oxford University Press, 2015), pp. 29-46.

Bacon, M., *Let This Life Speak: The Legacy of Henry Joel Cadbury* (Philadelphia: University of Pennsylvania Press, 1987).

Bacon, M., *Mothers of Feminism: The Story of Quaker Women in America* (New York: Harper & Row, 1989).

Bacon, M., *The Quiet Rebels: The Story of the Quakers in America* (New York: Basic Books, 1969).

Bacon, M., *Valiant Friend: The Life of Lucretia Mott* (New York: Walker and Company1980).

Bailyn, B. *Education in the Forming of American Society* (New York: W.W. Norton, 1972).

Baltzell, E., *Puritan Boston and Quaker Philadelphia* (New York: Free Press, 1979).

Barbour, H., *The Quakers in Puritan England* (New Haven, CT: Yale University Press, 1964).

Barbour, H., "The Young Controversialist," in *The World of William Penn*, edited by R. Dunn and M. Dunn, editors, (Philadelphia: University of Pennsylvania Press, 1986), pp. 15-29.

Barbour, H., and Frost, J., *The Quakers* (Westport, CT: Greenwood Press, 1988).

Beers, D., "The Centennial City, 1865–1876," R. Weigley, editor, *Philadelphia: A 300-Year History* (New York: W.W. Norton & Company 1982), pp. 417-470.

Benjamin, P., *The Quakers in the Industrial Age, 1865–1920* (Philadelphia: Temple University Press, 1976).

Berlin, I., *Generations of Captivity: A History of African American Slaves* (Cambridge, MA: Harvard University Press, 2003).

Boorstin, D., *The Americans: The Colonial Experience* (New York: Random House, 1958).

Braithwaite, W., *The Beginnings of Quakerism* (London: Macmillan and Company, 1912).

Brandt, N., and Yanna, K., *In the Shadow of the Civil War: Passmore Williamson and the Rescue of Jane Johnson* (Columbia: University of South Carolina Press, 2007).

Brinton, H., *The Religious Philosophy of Quakerism* (Wallingford, PA: Pendle Hill Press, 1973).

Brock, P., *The Quaker Peace Testimony, 1660–1914* (York, England: William Sessions, 1990).

Bronner, E., "A Time of Change: Philadelphia Yearly Meeting, 1861–1914," in J. Moore, editor. *Friends in the Delaware Valley: Philadelphia Yearly Meeting, 1681–1981* (Haverford, PA: Friends Historical Association, 1981), pp. 103-137.

Bronner, E., "*Village into Town, 1701–1746*," in *Philadelphia: A 300-Year History*, edited by Russell F. Weigley (New York: W.W. Norton & Company, 1982), pp. 43-52.

Bronner, E., *William Penn's "Holy Experiment": The Founding of Pennsylvania, 1681–1701* (Westport, CT: Greenwood Press, 1978).

Bronner, E., and Fraser, D., *William Penn's Published Writings, 1660–1726. An Interpretive Bibliography* (Philadelphia: University of Pennsylvania, 1986).

Burkhart, J., and West, R., "*… better than riches*": *A Tricentennial History of William Penn Charter School* (Philadelphia: William Penn Charter School, 1989).

Burt, N. and Davies, W., "The Iron Age, 1876–1905," in R. Weigley. editor, *Philadelphia: A 300-Year History* (New York: W.W. Norton & Company 1982), pp. 471-523.

Cadbury, H., "The Hunt for Lincoln's Quaker Ancestors," *Friends Journal*. Vol. 12, No. 3, pp. 57-58 (Philadelphia: Religious Society of Friends, February 1, 1966).

Cadbury, H., "Negro Membership in the Society of Friends," *Journal of Negro History*, Vol. 21 No. 2, pp. 151-213 (Chicago: University of Chicago Press, April 1936).

Chapman, S., "Shot From Guns: The Lost Pacifism of American Quakers," *The New Republic* Vol. 180, No. 21, pp. 27-36 (June 9, 1979).

Cherry, C., *A Quiet Haven: Quakers, Moral Treatment, and Asylum Reform* (Teaneck, NJ: Fairleigh-Dickinson University Press, 1989).

Cimbala, P. and Miller, R., editors. *The Freedmen's Bureau and Reconstruction* (New York: Fordham University Press, 1999).

Colon, W., Heriza, T., and Histand, T., "Love in Action: A Brief History of AFSC's Work in the Past 100 Years" (May 18, 2017), AFSC.org

Densmore, C., "'Be Ye Therefore Perfect': Anti-Slavery and the and the Origins of the Yearly Meeting of Progressive Friends in Chester County, Pennsylvania," *Quaker History*, Vol. 93, No. 2, pp. 28-46 (Haverford, PA: Friends Historical Association, Fall 2004).

Doherty, R., *The Hicksite Separation: A Sociological Analysis of Religious Schism in Early Nineteenth-Century America* (New Brunswick, NJ: Rutgers University Press, 1967).

Drake, T., *Quakers and Slavery in America* (Gloucester, MA: Peter Smith, 1965).

Drinker, S., *Hannah Penn and the Proprietorship of Pennsylvania* (Philadelphia: National Society of the Colonial Dames of America in Pennsylvania, 1958).

Dunn, M., "The Personality of William Penn," in *The World of William Penn*, edited by R. Dunn and M. Dunn, editors, (Philadelphia: University of Pennsylvania Press, 1986), pp. 3-14.

Dunn, M., *William Penn: Politics and Conscience* (Princeton, NJ: Princeton University Press, 1967).

Dunn, R., "Penny Wise and Pound Foolish: Penn as a Businessman," in *The World of William Penn*, edited by R. Dunn and M. Dunn, editors (Philadelphia: University of Pennsylvania Press, 1986), pp. 37-54.

Dunn, R., and Dunn, M., R. Dunn and M. Dunn, editors, *The World of William Penn* (Philadelphia: University of Pennsylvania Press, 1986).

Engs, R., and Miller, R., editors, *The Birth of the Grand Old Party: The Republicans' First Generation* (Philadelphia: University of Pennsylvania Press, 2002).

Fager, C., "AFSC & Quakers: The Background of a Concern," *A Friendly Letter*, June 19, 2010, afriendlyletter.com/afsc-quakers-i-the-background-of-a-concern/.

Fager, C., editor, *Quaker Service at the Crossroads* (Bellefonte, PA: Kimo Press, 1988).

Faulkner, C., *Lucretia Mott's Heresy: Abolition and Women's Rights in Nineteenth-Century America* (Philadelphia: University of Pennsylvania Press, 2011).

Fischer, D., *Albion's Seed: Four British Folkways on America* (New York: Oxford University Press, 1991 paperback edition).

Fitzgerald, K., and Reinhardt, E., "The Legacy and Philanthropy of Anna Thomas Jeanes," *Friends Journal Online* (March 1, 2020), www.friendsjournal.org/the-legacy-and-philanthropy-of-anna-thomas-jeanes/.

Flanagan, C., "Private Schools Have Become Truly Obscene," *The Atlantic*, April 2021, www.theatlantic.com/magazine/archive/2021/04/private-schools-are-indefensible/618078/.

Foner, E., "The Ideology of the Republican Party," in R. Engs and R. Miller, editors, *The Birth of the Grand Old Party: The Republicans' First Generation* (Philadelphia: University of Pennsylvania Press, 2002), pp. 8-28.

Frost, J., *A Perfect Freedom: Religious Liberty in Pennsylvania* (University Park, PA: Penn State Press, 1993).

Frost, J., *The Keithian Controversy in Early Pennsylvania* (Norwood, PA: Norwood Editions, 1980).

Frost, J., "'Our Deeds Carry Our Message': The Early History of the American Friends Service Committee," *Quaker History*, Vol. 81, No. 1, pp. 1-50 (Haverford, PA: Friends Historical Association, Spring 1992).

Frost, J., "'Wear the Sword As Long As Thou Canst': William Penn in Myth and History," *Explorations in Early American Culture*, Vol. 4, *pp. 13-45* (Philadelphia: University of Pennsylvania Press, 2000).

Gerbner, K., "'We Are Against the Traffik of Men-Body': The Germantown Quaker Protest of 1688 and the Origins of American Abolitionism," *Pennsylvania History*. Vol. 74, No. 2, pp. 149-172 (University Park: Penn State Press, Spring 2007).

Godbeer, R., *World of Trouble: A Philadelphia Quaker Family's Journey through the American Revolution* (New Haven, CT: Yale University Press, 2019).

Guelzo, A., *Abraham Lincoln: Redeemer President* (Grand Rapids, MI: William B. Eerdmans Publishing Company, 1999).

Gurney, G., "Alexander Milne Calder: William Penn," *in Fairmount Park Art Association, Sculpture of a City: Philadelphia's Treasures in Bronze and Stone* (New York: Walker, 1974), pp. 104-109.

Hadley, H., "Diminishing Separation: Philadelphia Yearly Meetings Reunite, 1915–1955," in J. Moore, editor, *Friends in the Delaware Valley: Philadelphia Yearly Meeting, 1681–1981* (Haverford, PA: Friends Historical Association, 1981), pp. 138-172.

Hamm, T., "Hicksite, Orthodox, and Evangelical Quakerism, 1805–1887," in S. Angel and P. Dandelion, editors, *Oxford Handbook of Quaker Studies* (New York: Oxford University Press, 2015), pp. 63-77.

Hamm, T., *The Quakers in America* (New York: Columbia University Press, 2003).

Hertz, E., *Lincoln Talks* (New York: Viking, 1939).

Hill, C., *The World Turned Upside Down: Radical Ideas During the English Revolution* (New York: Penguin Books, 1985).

Hogan, D., "The Market Revolution and Disciplinary Power: Joseph Lancaster and the Psychology of the Early Classroom System," *History of Education Quarterly*. Vol. 29, No. 3, pp. 381-417 (Cambridge, UK: Cambridge University Press, Fall 1989).

Holland, J., "'Snowplow Parents' and the Pressure at Top Private Schools," *Washingtonian*, October 9, 2011, www.washingtonian.com/2011/10/09/snowplow-parents-and-the-pressure-at-top-private-schools/.

Illick, J., *William Penn the Politician* (Ithaca, New York: Cornell University Press, 1965).

Ingle, H., *First Among Friends: George Fox & the Creation of Quakerism* (New York: Oxford University Press, 1994).

Ingle, H., *Quakers in Conflict: The Hicksite Reformation* (Knoxville: University of Tennessee Press, 1986).

Jackson, M., *Let This Voice Be Heard: Anthony Benezet, Father of Atlantic Abolitionism* (Philadelphia: University of Pennsylvania Press, 2009).

James, S., *A People Among Peoples: Quaker Benevolence in Eighteenth-Century America* (Cambridge, MA: Harvard University Press, 1963).

Jennings, F., "Brother Miquon: Good Lord!" in R. Dunn and M. Dunn, editors, *The World of William Penn* (Philadelphia: University of Pennsylvania Press, 1986), p.198.

Johnston, N., *Eastern State Penitentiary: Crucible of Good Intentions* (Philadelphia: Philadelphia Museum of Art, 1994).

Jones, M., "Philadelphia Yearly Meeting and the American Friends Service Committee," in J. Moore, editor, *Friends in the Delaware Valley: Philadelphia Yearly Meeting, 1681–1981* (Haverford, PA: Friends Historical Association, 1981), pp. 234-247.

Jones, M., *Swords into Ploughshares: An Account of the American Friends Service Committee, 1917–1937* (New York: Macmillan, 1937).

Jones, R., *A Service of Love in Wartime: American Friends Relief Work in Europe, 1917–1919* (New York: Macmillan, 1920).

Jones, R., *The Quakers in the American Colonies* (London: Macmillan, 1911).

Kashatus, W., *A Virtuous Education: William Penn's Vision for Philadelphia's Schools* (Wallingford, PA: Pendle Hill Press, 1997).

Kashatus, W., *Abraham Lincoln, the Quakers and Civil War: A Trial of Faith and Principle* (Santa Barbara, CA: Praeger, 2014).

Kashatus, W., "A Reappraisal of Anthony Benezet's Activities in Educational Reform, 1754–1784," *Quaker History*, Vol. 78, No. 1, pp. 24-36 (Haverford, PA: Friends Historical Association, Spring 1989).

Kashatus, W., *Conflict of Conviction: A Reappraisal of Quaker Involvement in the American Revolution* (Lanham, MD: University Press of America, 1990).

Kashatus, W., "Friends Fight for Freedom," *Pennsylvania Heritage*, Vol. XIV, No. 3, pp. 4-9 (Harrisburg: Pennsylvania Historical and Museum Commission, Summer 1988).

Kashatus, W., "Images of William Penn: An Evolving Portrait of Pennsylvania's Founding Father," in *An Image of Peace: The Penn Treaty Collection of Mr. and Mrs. Meyer P. Potamkin* (Harrisburg: Pennsylvania Museum and Historical Commission, 1996), pp. 7-16.

Kashatus, W., *Just Over the Line: Chester County and the Underground Railroad* (West Chester, PA: Chester County Historical Society & Penn State Press, 2002).

Kashatus, W., *William Still: The Underground Railroad and the Angel at Philadelphia* (South Bend, IN: Notre Dame University Press, 2021).

Keiser, D., "Quaker Ancestors of Lincoln," *Lincoln Herald*, Vol. 63, No. 3, pp. 134-137 (Harrogate, TN: Abraham Lincoln Library & Museum, 1961).

Kelsey, R., *Friends and the Indians, 1655–1917* (Philadelphia: Executive Committee of Friends on Indian Affairs, 1917).

Krugler, J., *English and Catholic: The Lords Baltimore in the Seventeenth Century* (Baltimore: Johns Hopkins University Press, 2004).

Labaree, D., *The Making of an American High School: The Credentials Market and the Central High School of Philadelphia, 1838–1939* (New Haven, CT: Yale University Press, 1988).

Lascroux, F., "The Toxic Influence of the Private School System," *Education International*, December 14, 2022, www.ei-ie.org/en/item/27172:the-toxic-influence-of-the-private-school-system.

Lewy, G., *Peace & Revolution: The Moral Crisis of American Pacifism* (Grand Rapids, MI: William B. Eerdmans, 1987).

Lippincott, H., *The History of Abington Meeting, 1697–1949* (Jenkintown, PA: Abington Monthly Meeting, 1950).

Marietta, J., *The Reformation of American Quakerism, 1748–1783* (Philadelphia: University of Pennsylvania Press, 1984).

Marietta, J. and Rowe, G., *Troubled Experiment: Crime and Justice in Pennsylvania, 1682–1800* (Philadelphia: University of Pennsylvania, 2006).

Mayer, H., *All on Fire: William Lloyd Garrison and the Abolition of Slavery* (New York: St. Martin's Press, 1998).

McCormick, D., "Can Quakerism Survive?" *Friends Journal* (February 2018), pp. 15-17

McDaniel, D., and Julye, V., *Fit for Freedom, Not for Friendship: Quakers, African Americans and the Myth of Racial Justice* (Philadelphia: Friends General Conference, 2009).

McGowan, J., *Station Master in the Underground Railroad: The Life and Letters of Thomas Garrett* (Jefferson, NC: McFarland & Company, 2005).

McPherson, J., *Battle Cry of Freedom: The Civil War Era* (New York: Oxford University Press, 1988).

McPherson, J., *Ordeal By Fire: The Civil War and Reconstruction* (New York: McGraw-Hill, 2001, 3rd edition).

Mekeel, A., "The Founding Years, 1681–1789," in *Friends in the Delaware Valley: Philadelphia Yearly Meeting, 1681–1981*, edited by J. Moore (Haverford, PA: Friends Historical Association, 1981), pp. 23-24.

Mekeel, A., *The Quakers and the American Revolution* (York, England: William Sessions, 1996).

Meranze, M., *Laboratories of Virtue: Punishment, Revolution and Authority in Philadelphia, 1760–1835* (Chapel Hill: University of North Carolina Press, 1996).

Miller, L., *Witness for Humanity: A Biography of Clarence E. Pickett* (Wallingford, PA: Pendle Hill Press, 1999).

Miller, R., "The Federal City, 1783–1800," in R. Weigley, editor, *Philadelphia: A 300-Year History* (New York: W.W. Norton & Company 1982), pp. 161-78.

Miller, R., and Marzik, T., editors. *Immigrants and Religion in Urban America* (Philadelphia: Temple University Press, 1977).

Milner, C., *With Good Intentions: Quaker Work among the Pawnees, Otos, and Omahas in 1870s* (Lincoln: University of Nebraska Press, 1982).

Murphy, A., *William Penn: A Life* (New York: Oxford University Press, 2019).

Moore, J., editor, *Friends in the Delaware Valley: Philadelphia Yearly Meeting, 1681–1981* (Haverford, PA: Friends Historical Association, 1981).

Nash, G., *Forging Freedom: The Formation of Philadelphia's Black Community, 1720–1840* (Cambridge, MA: Harvard University, 1988).

Nash, G., and Soderlund, J., *Freedom By Degrees: Emancipation in Pennsylvania and its Aftermath* (New York: Oxford University Press, 1991).

Nash, G., *The Liberty Bell* (New Haven, CT: Yale University Press, 2010).

Powell, J., *Bring Out Your Dead: The Great Plague of Yellow Fever in Philadelphia in 1793* (Philadelphia: no publisher, 1949).

Ream, M., "Philadelphia Friends and the Indians," in J. Moore, editor, *Friends in the Delaware Valley: Philadelphia Yearly Meeting, 1681–1981* (Haverford, PA: Friends Historical Association, 1981), pp. 200-214.

Rediker, M., *The Fearless Benjamin Lay: The Quaker Dwarf Who Became the First Revolutionary Abolitionist* (Boston: Beacon, 2017).

Rothman, D., *The Discovery of the Asylum: Social Order & Disorder in the New Republic* (Boston: Little Brown & Company, 1971).

Scharf, J., and Thompson, W., *History of Philadelphia, 1609–1884* (3 vols., Philadelphia: no publisher, 1884).

Scranton, P., *Proprietary Capitalism: The Textile Manufacture at Philadelphia, 1800–1885* (Cambridge, England: Cambridge University Press, 2003).

Sharp, A., "Victims of Two Enemies: The Quakers in the Civil War," *Evangelical Friend* Vol. 11, No. 3, pp. 6-7 (Alliance, OH: Evangelical Friends Alliance, November 1978).

Sheeran, M., *Beyond Majority Rule: Voteless Decisions in the Religious Society of Friends* (Philadelphia: Philadelphia Yearly Meeting, 1996).

Sheppard, W., editor, *William Penn's Colony: Passengers and Ships, Prior to 1684* (Baltimore: Genealogical Publishing Company, 1970).

Soderlund, J., *Separate Paths: Lenapes and Colonists in West New Jersey* (New Brunswick, NJ: Rutgers University Press, 2022).

Soderlund, J., *Lenape Country: Delaware Valley Society Before William Penn* (Philadelphia: University of Pennsylvania Press, 2015).

Soderlund, J., *Quakers & Slavery: A Divided Spirit* (Princeton: Princeton University, 1985).

Spears, L., "Servant-Leadership and Quakers," *Quaker Life*, (July–August 2003), pp. 5-7.

Suppinger, J., "The Intimate Lincoln," *Lincoln Herald*, Vol. 85, No. 3, p. 161 (Harrogate, TN: Abraham Lincoln Library & Museum, Fall 1983).

Teeters, N., "The Early Days of Eastern State Penitentiary at Philadelphia," *Pennsylvania History*. Vol. 16, No. 3, pp. 261-302 (University Park, PA: Penn State Press, October 1949).

Tolles, F., *Meeting House and Counting House: The Quaker Merchants of Colonial Philadelphia, 1682–1763* (New York: W.W. Norton, 1948).

Treese, L., *The Storm Gathering: The Penn Family and the American Revolution* (University Park, PA: Penn State Press, 1992).

Trussell, J., *William Penn: Architect of a Nation* (Harrisburg: Pennsylvania Historical and Museum Commission, 1983).

Vaux, G., "The Embarkation, Voyage and Arrival of the Ship 'Welcome,' 1682," in *Bulletin of the Friends Historical Association*, Vol. 21, No. 2, pp. 59-62 (Philadelphia: Friends Historical Association, Autumn 1932).

Vipont, E., *George Fox and the Valiant Sixty* (London: Hamish Hamilton, 1975).

Wahl, A., "The Progressive Friends of Longwood," *Friends Historical Society Bulletin* 42, No. 1, pp. 14-16 (Philadelphia: Friends Historical Society, Spring 1953).

Wainwright, N., "Age of Nicholas Biddle, 1825–1854," in R. Weigley, editor, *Philadelphia: A 300-Year History* (New York: W.W. Norton & Company 1982), pp. 258-306.

Weber, J., "'If Ever War Was Holy': Quaker Soldiers and the Union Army," *North and South*, Vol. 5, No. 5, pp. 60-72 (Tollhouse, CA: The Civil War Society, April 2002).

Weigley. R., editor, *Philadelphia: A 300-Year History* (New York: W.W. Norton & Company 1982).

Weslager, C., *The Delaware Indians*. (New Brunswick, NJ: Rutgers University Press, 2000).

Wetherill, C., *History of the Religious Society of Friends Called by Some the Free Quakers in the City of Philadelphia* (Philadelphia: no publisher, 1894).

Wildes, H., *William Penn: A Biography* (New York: Macmillan, 1974).

Wilson, R., *Philadelphia Quakers, 1681–1981* (Philadelphia: Philadelphia Yearly Meeting of the Religious Society of Friends, 1981).

Wilson, R., *Quaker Relief: An Account of the Relief Work of the Society of Friends, 1940–1948* (London: Allen & Unwin, 1952).

Wolf, E., *Philadelphia: Portrait of an American City* (Philadelphia: Camino Press & The Library Company of Philadelphia, 1990).

Woody, T., *Early Quaker Education in Pennsylvania* (New York: Teacher's College, Columbia University, 1920).

Zuckerman, M., editor, *Friends and Neighbors: Group Life in America's First Plural Society* (Philadelphia: Temple University Press, 1982).

Zuckerman, M., *Peaceable Kingdoms. New England Towns in the Eighteenth Century* (New York: Alfred A. Knopf, 1970).

About the Author

William C. Kashatus is a Quaker historian, educator, and author. A product of and former teacher in Philadelphia's Friends Schools, Kashatus graduated Phi Beta Kappa from Earlham College. He earned his master's degree in history from Brown University and his doctorate from the University of Pennsylvania. His published works include *William Still: The Underground Railroad and the Angel at Philadelphia* (2021); *Abraham Lincoln, the Quakers and the Civil War* (2014); *A Virtuous Education: William Penn's Vision for Philadelphia's Schools* (1997); and *Conflict of Conviction: A Reappraisal of Quaker Involvement in the American Revolution* (1990).

Endorsements

William Kashatus provides a concise and accurate history of the impact of Quakers on Philadelphia from its founding by William Penn until the present. He draws upon his own earlier publications on Quakers and Lincoln, Chester County, and the American Revolution and shows how Friends pioneered efforts for freedom of religion, antislavery, women's rights, social justice, and peace.

J. William Frost, author of *A Perfect Freedom: Religious Liberty in Pennsylvania*

In *Philadelphia Quakers: A Brief History*, William Kashatus shows how a people few in numbers but big in purpose did much to shape the character and conduct of Philadelphia, and beyond. The genius of Kashatus's book is its honesty in relating the tensions among Philadelphia Quakers who knew they must live in the world, and improve it, without becoming of the world and a slave to it. *Philadelphia Quakers* is at once a compelling American story of a people in a constant state of becoming and an invitation to consider how and why faith-based people make history by the institutions they build and the causes they compel.

Randall M. Miller, co-editor of *Pennsylvania: A History of the Commonwealth*

Philadelphia Quakers have always been few in number. But, pound for pound, they have been the most culturally creative religious community in all of American history. They have led the nation in promoting popular democracy, religious pluralism, the empowerment of women, the abolition of slavery, and much more. In this brief but luminous book, William

Kashatus tells their story as it has never been told before. Kashatus, a longtime Quaker, writes lovingly of his people and admiringly of their astonishing accomplishments yet never neglects their foibles and failings. No one knows their past better. No one ponders their present and future with more urgency.

Michael Zuckerman, author of *Peaceable Kingdoms: New England Towns in the Eighteenth Century*